6/21/22
5

N/C
5-19

P9-CEJ-014

INSIGHT ⊙ GUIDES

EXPLORE

DUBROVNIK

⦿ Walking Eye App

YOUR FREE EBOOK AVAILABLE THROUGH THE WALKING EYE APP

Your guide now includes a free eBook to your chosen destination, for the same great price as before. Simply download the Walking Eye App from the App Store or Google Play to access your free eBook.

HOW THE WALKING EYE APP WORKS

Through the Walking Eye App, you can purchase a range of eBooks and destination content. However, when you buy this book, you can download the corresponding eBook for free. Just see below in the grey panel where to find your free content and then scan the QR code at the bottom of this page.

Destinations: Download essential destination content featuring recommended sights and attractions, restaurants, hotels and an A–Z of practical information, all available for purchase.

Ships: Interested in ship reviews? Find independent reviews of river and ocean ships in this section, all available for purchase.

eBooks: You can download your free accompanying digital version of this guide here. You will also find a whole range of other eBooks, all available for purchase.

Free access to travel-related blog articles about different destinations, updated on a daily basis.

HOW THE EBOOKS WORK

The eBooks are provided in EPUB file format. Please note that you will need an eBook reader installed on your device to open the file. Many devices come with this as standard, but you may still need to install one manually from Google Play.

The eBook content is identical to the content in the printed guide.

HOW TO DOWNLOAD THE WALKING EYE APP

1. Download the Walking Eye App from the App Store or Google Play.
2. Open the app and select the scanning function from the main menu.
3. Scan the QR code on this page – you will then be asked a security question to verify ownership of the book.
4. Once this has been verified, you will see your eBook in the purchased ebook section, where you will be able to download it.

Other destination apps and eBooks are available for purchase separately or are free with the purchase of the Insight Guide book.

CONTENTS

BACK TO NATURE

Revel in the greenery of the National Park in Mljet (route 8) where you can hire a bike. Lokrum's trails lead through lush botanical gardens and a saltwater lagoon (route 6).

RECOMMENDED ROUTES FOR...

BEST VIEWS

A walk around the City Walls (route 1) is a must. Take the cable car to Mount Srđ (route 4) for sweeping views. Head out to Lapad (route 5) for glimpses of the Elaphite Islands.

ESCAPING THE CROWDS

Hop on a boat to pretty Cavtat (route 9) for a walk around the peninsula. Take a short drive to Zaton (route 10) on the way to Trsteno for a waterside lunch.

FOODIES

Head out to Mali Ston (route 10) for what are regarded as the best oysters in Croatia. Spend a day in Korčula (route 11) and sample some of the region's top wines.

HISTORY BUFFS

Breathtaking and beautifully preserved Renaissance architecture surrounds you on a wander through the Old Town (route 2). Hike up to Fort Lovrijenac after exploring the historic City Walls (route 1).

ISLAND HOPPING

Choose from a short jaunt to Lokrum (route 6) or a longer trip to the Elaphite Islands (route 7) or Mljet (route 8). If you want to go further afield, spend the night in Korčula (route 11).

SEASIDE FUN

Clamber among the rocks and pebbly beaches of Lapad and Babin Kuk (route 5). Banje (route 4) is the city's beach, with great views of the old port.

STREET LIFE

Join the strollers along the main Stradun thoroughfare (route 2) and take in the lively atmosphere of the tiny bars squeezed into the narrow lanes leading up to Prijeko (route 3).

INTRODUCTION

An introduction to Dubrovnik's geography, customs and culture, plus illuminating background information on cuisine, history and what to do when you're there.

EXPLORE DUBROVNIK

Behind the fairy-tale façade of Dubrovnik's medieval walls lies a city of inexhaustible beauty. It's as beguiling now as when Lord Byron clapped eyes on it two centuries ago and called it the 'Pearl of the Adriatic'.

Framed by the deep blue waters of the Adriatic Sea, the glittering former Republic of Ragusa enjoys one of the most dramatic settings along Croatia's Dalmatian coast. Dubrovnik was once a powerful maritime trading port, and this Unesco World Heritage Site still shows an independent spirit born of centuries of keeping an eye on its enemies with a clever combination of diplomacy and hefty fortifications.

Within its medieval protective walls are shimmering marble streets lined with green-shuttered stone houses. Its two most impressive buildings – the Rector's Palace and Sponza Palace – survived the devastating earthquake of 1667 that destroyed much of its Venetian Gothic and Renaissance architecture. The remade baroque city took another battering as recently as 1991, when Serbian and Montenegrin forces besieged Dubrovnik during the bitter Yugoslav civil war. With admirable speed, the city was repaired once again, showing few scars apart from the tell-tale brightness of newer terracotta roof tiles.

Nowadays, the only sieges are from the large groups of cruise passengers and coach parties that throng the streets during the day. Come late afternoon, the café tables that fill the lanes and squares hum with contented coffee drinkers happy to reclaim the city from the day-trippers. Warm summer evenings bring a magical ambience, with music drifting from classical concerts being held in historic buildings. In the many outdoor restaurants, diners feast on plates of fresh seafood before they head off to the bars tucked into the narrow streets off Stradun.

GEOGRAPHY AND LAYOUT

Dubrovnik is on Croatia's southeastern tip, just 37km (23 miles) from the border with Montenegro. A forbidding ridge of bare brown mountains flanks its northern side, a stark contrast to the vibrant blue of the Adriatic Sea. The Elaphite Islands and Mljet are to the northwest, and beyond those are the fertile vineyards and villages of the Pelješac peninsula.

Dubrovnik

Although the Old Town is the major focus for most visitors, it occupies a

Dubrovnik's picturesque harbour

geographically small portion of the city. The area of Ploče, where grand hotels overlook the coast and the town beach, is to the east. The workaday port of Gruž hugs the coast to the west, and the Lapad and Babin Kuk peninsulas hive off slightly southwards. The latter two are where many of the family-oriented hotels are based, as they're close to the main beaches. Gruž, Lapad and Babin Kuk are all connected to the fully pedestrianised Old Town by an efficient network of buses. Boats make regular 15-minute trips from the Old Town's harbour to the tiny island of Lokrum, which manages to squeeze in a monastery, saltwater lake, botanical gardens and rocky beaches.

Day trips from Dubrovnik

Dubrovnik makes a good base for visiting the nearby islands and villages. Regular ferries and catamarans leave from Gruž harbour to the island of Mljet and the Elaphite archipelago of Lopud, Šipan and Koločep. Further afield is the island of Korčula, which can be combined with a road trip to Mali Ston on the Pelješac peninsula to sample the village's renowned oysters.

South of Dubrovnik is the village of Cavtat, which juts out on a peninsula that can be reached by boat or by bus. This is part of the Konavle region, the last Croatian one before Montenegro, and home to vineyards and numerous bicycle trails through hills and valleys.

Beyond Dubrovnik

There's no shortage of tour companies in Dubrovnik offering day excursions to its two foreign neighbours. Mostar in Bosnia-Herzegovina is about a two-hour drive away, and it's an even shorter journey to reach the beautiful village of Kotor in Montenegro. Buses to Split further north along the Adriatic coast take about four hours.

HISTORY

For such a tiny place Dubrovnik has a fascinating history. There were signs of a settlement as early as the 6th century. Over the centuries it was taken over by the Byzantines, the Venetians, the Hungarians and the French. The first recorded mention of the Republic of Ragusa was in 1181; by the 16th century, the city had a powerful merchant navy with more than 200 vessels that traded all over the known world. It started to decline in the 17th century when the English and the Dutch grew in strength, and the republic was finally dissolved in 1808 when Napoleon invaded.

When Yugoslavia started to disintegrate and war broke out between Serbs and Croats, Dubrovnik was besieged in October 1991. The port at Gruž and the airport were destroyed, and the Old City subjected to mortar attack. Almost 100 civilians were killed in Dubrovnik and numerous buildings damaged, but a major reconstruction exercise has restored the city.

View from the City Walls

Art and architecture

The 15th and 16th centuries were a prosperous time, when the Republic flourished both commercially and artistically. Although the Dubrovnik School is not widely known outside Croatia, its artists produced a sound body of work. Much of their output was destroyed in the fire that followed the earthquake of 1667, but some can still be seen. Three works by Nikola Božidarević (1464–1517) are in the Dominican Monastery Museum, which also displays a richly textured *Baptism of Christ*, by Lovro Dobričević (1420–78); his portrait of St Blaise is in the Franciscan Monastery and a polyptych in the Dnče church. Another *Baptism of Christ*, this one by Mihajlo Hamzić (died c. 1518), can be found in the Rector's Palace.

Architecture also blossomed during the Italian Renaissance, spearheaded by the Florentine Michelozzo Michelozzi; it was in the 15th century that some of the city's most splendid buildings were built or embellished. Most were destroyed by the earthquake, and what didn't survive was rebuilt in the baroque style that now dominates the Old Town.

CLIMATE

Average temperatures in winter (November–February) range from 8–12°C (46–54°F), April, May and October 14–18°C (57–65°F), June and September 21–22°C (70–72°F), July–August 24–25°C (75–77°F), although summer highs can soar up to 30°C (86°F). The best times to visit Dubrovnik are May–June and September–October. The weather should be fine and sunny and the sea is usually still warm in the autumn. The town will be less crowded, accommodation easier to find and flights will be cheaper. Dubrovnik can be lovely on a crisp, cold winter day, especially during the Christmas market in December. But there

---

Festive February

You can't be in Dubrovnik for long without realising that St Blaise (Sveti Vlaho) is the city's patron saint. Not only does his image appear over the Pile and Ploče Gates flanking the Old Town, but he also has his own church and his relics are kept in the Cathedral Treasury. This Armenian bishop, who was martyred in the 3rd century, is celebrated in exuberant style in early February, bringing cheer to an otherwise gloomy month. Two days of festivities attract thousands of people to the streets of the Old Town to watch the colourful processions. Flags and banners cover the buildings, and national costumes are dusted off as everyone joins in the two days of music, dancing and feasting.

The party doesn't end there. Depending on when Easter falls, the pre-Lenten carnival usually takes place at some point in February. Cue more music, dancing and general merry-making.

Korčula ferry captain

are wet and windy days too, and flight schedules taper off during the winter. Many restaurants hotels close, and few, if any, boats run to the islands.

POPULATION

The population of Dubrovnik is about 43,000. The vast majority are Croats, with small groups of Muslims and Serbs as well as a tiny Jewish population. Over recent years, there has been an increase of people with Croatian backgrounds who have emigrated to the city to run businesses. There has also been a return of residents who had left Dubrovnik during the conflict of the early 1990s. Because so much of the city revolves around tourism, there is a large population of young people working in the bars, shops and restaurants.

DON'T LEAVE DUBROVNIK WITHOUT...

Walking the City Walls. Get a glimpse of daily life in the Old Town and absorb the city's history by walking around these magnificent medieval fortifications. See page 30.

Having a sundowner at Buža Bar. Watch the sun go down from this simple little bar that clings to the side of the cliff below the City Walls. Look out for the sign that says 'Cold drinks with the most beautiful view'. That's exactly what you get – plastic cups and all. See page 47.

Going up to Mount Srđ. Some of best views not only of the city but also the surrounding countryside and the coastline can be seen from the top of this mountain looming over Dubrovnik. You can ride the cable car, take an hour-long hike or combine the two. See page 52.

Eating the 'world's best oysters'. Back in 1936, the oysters from the nearby village of Mali Ston were given this accolade at the General Trades International Exhibition in London. Hyperbole or not, the oysters certainly are delicious and can be found on many menus in Dubrovnik as well as in Ston on the Pelješac peninsula. See page 78.

Discovering recent history. The excellent War Photo Limited gallery has a permanent exhibition of photographs covering the Balkans conflict as well as temporary displays of compelling war photography from around the world. See page 45.

Escaping the city for a day. Take the 15-minute ferry from the Old Port to the small island of Lokrum, where you can wander through wooded trails and botanical gardens, take a dip in a saltwater lagoon or go swimming off the rocks. See page 58.

Watching the sunset from Park Orsula. Just south of the city is an amphitheatre that's become the venue for the Orsuladanja summer music festival. But you don't need to be there for the festival to catch breathtaking views of the sun setting over the Old Port. See page 23.

Dubrovnik viewed from above

People and customs

Dalmatians often resemble their Italian neighbours across the Adriatic, mainly in their manners and attitudes towards fashion: they do like to be smartly dressed. They even do their own version of the Italian *passeggiata* called the *džir*, when people signal the end of a working day by strolling leisurely down the main pedestrianised street Stradun, stopping for a coffee and – most importantly – people-watching.

Unlike their Italian neighbours, however, shopkeepers and restaurateurs in Dubrovnik tend to keep their businesses open throughout the day, without the customary Italian three-hour closing. Most museums are closed on Monday, with a few closed on Tuesday instead, but the City Walls are open every day.

RELIGION

Croatia is an overwhelmingly Roman Catholic country, and church attendance soared immediately after independence in 1991. It has tailed off considerably since then, although there is still a great deal of enthusiasm for the many religious festivals held throughout the year.

TOURISM

Tourism is the mainstay of the local economy, and increases every year. However, the relentless rise of the cruise industry and package coach tours means that the city is quite overwhelmed for much of the day during the summer.

The standard of English spoken by people in the tourism industry is very high, particularly among younger people. But people of all ages switch easily between the main languages being spoken by tourists in Dubrovnik, namely English, Italian and German.

POLITICS AND ECONOMICS

Since Croatia joined the European Union in 2013, its economy has been shrinking as it has been unable to generate much business outside of the tourism industry. Its expensive, bulky and bureaucracy-laden public sector continues to drain money from the economy, something that the government has been very slow to rectify.

Croatia's current head of government is Prime Minister Andrej Plenković, who is the leader of the conservative centre-right Croatian Democratic Union (HDZ). The current head of state is President Kolinda Grabar-Kitarović, the first woman to hold this post. Mayor of Dubrovnik until 2017, left-of-centre Andro Vlahušić voiced his concerns about the fact that his city, like its former master Venice across the Adriatic, was becoming a city too expensive for locals to live in. During his tenure he devised various programmes to entice young graduates to return to the city

Korčula Town is only a hop away

once they had finished their studies elsewhere. His successor, Mato Franković of the conservative HDZ party, made the radical decision to drastically cut the daily number of tourists allowed inside the City Walls to 8,000 people. And there are plans to further reduce this number to 4,000.

TOP TIPS FOR EXPLORING DUBROVNIK

Stradun in season. In the height of summer, when as many as six cruise ships have disgorged their passengers, Stradun can become a barely moving sea of people. This is the time for you to explore quieter parts of the city or one of the islands. The cruise crowds will have left by about 4pm, so that's the time to have a more leisurely stroll and stop for a coffee.

Dubrovnik Card. If you're there for more than a day and plan to do some sightseeing, the Dubrovnik Card will pay for itself very quickly. The tourist pass includes entry to most attractions – including the City Walls – as well as free buses and restaurant discounts.

Gruž market. Dubrovnik's biggest and most authentic food market takes place every morning near the Jadrolinja ferry port. It's a lively affair, full of residents stocking up on fresh produce. There's a smaller daily market in Gundulić Square in the Old Town, which, after locals do their shopping first thing in the morning, becomes more of a tourist attraction.

Bring swimming shoes. Although there are sandy beaches on some of the nearby islands, the ones in Dubrovnik are either pebbly or rocky. If your feet are sensitive, you're better off wearing protective shoes. You can find these easily in local beach shops if you don't bring your own.

Get to know the islands. It's very easy to take boats, ferries and catamarans to nearby islands including Mljet, the Elaphite archipelago and Korčula, although crossings tend to peter out from November to March. Some of the islands, notably Korčula, are worth an overnight stay.

Arriving from the airport. The airport transfer is straightforward, efficient and very cheap. A single fare is about a 10th the price of a taxi, which wouldn't be allowed into the car-free Old Town anyway. Buses are timed to coincide with each flight and will drop you off outside the Pile Gate.

Get lost and look up. The Old Town is packed with narrow streets, many of which lead up and down stairs to hidden flower-filled courtyards and into tiny stone arcades. It's a delight just to wander and explore, and especially to look up and spot one fascinating architectural detail after another.

Summer Festival. At the height of the season for about six weeks in July and August, the Summer Festival fills the streets of the Old Town night after night after the daily tourists have gone home. It does get extremely busy, and you have to book accommodation well in advance, but it is an incredible spectacle.

Lobster pasta

FOOD AND DRINK

For a relatively small city, Dubrovnik has an enviable range of restaurants offering a mouth-watering selection of fresh fish, seafood and succulent meats. And within its narrow streets are a few culinary surprises.

The growth of the cruise industry in Dubrovnik has brought with it higher prices than you'll find in most parts of Croatia, and some of the more touristy places take advantage of the fact that they're unlikely to see these customers again. But this same influx has prompted many restaurateurs to up their game and devise more creative dishes. You're likely to find a stronger international flavour mingling with traditional Dalmatian cuisine – for example, with more Asian influences being adapted successfully.

LOCAL CUISINE

The Italian influence is unmistakable in Dubrovnik's cuisine, which features an almost dizzying array of pasta and risotto dishes. But seafood is the star, which you'll find in most restaurants – even some pizzerias. The word for fish is *riba*, and varieties range from gilt-head bream (*orada*), red mullet (*trilja*) and sea bream (*arbun*) to the humbler mackerel (*skuše*), sardines (*srdele*) and anchovies (*inćuni*), all excellent when simply grilled and served with a salad.

Seafood

Prevalent on Dubrovnik's menus is shellfish (*školjke*), including mussels, which rather confusingly are known both as *mušule* and *dagnje*, shrimps (*račiće*) and Dublin Bay prawns (*škampi*). You will often see *mušule na buzaru* or *bouzara*, which means the molluscs are cooked with wine, parsley, garlic (lots) and breadcrumbs; some versions also include tomatoes. Squid (*lignji*) and octopus (*hobotnica*) also appear on most menus, cooked in a variety of ways: fried (*prigani* or *pržene*), grilled (*na žaru*) or stuffed (*punjeni*). One of the most popular dishes is a simple octopus salad with garlic and olive oil.

On more upmarket menus you may find lobster (*jastog*) or oysters (*oštrige*): the former is more prevalent on the island of Mljet, the latter up the coast in Ston and Mali Ston, where the best oysters are farmed.

Meat

Meat lovers should not despair. As well as the tasty Dalmatian smoked ham (*dalmatinski pršut*), similar to prosciutto, that appears as a first course on

The popular octopus salad

Seafood platter

most menus, there is usually chicken breast (*pileća prsa*) or chicken escalope (*pileći file*) and pork cutlets (*svinjski kutlet*) as well as steak (simply called *biftek*) and platters of grilled meats.

On some of the nearby islands, restaurants specialise in cooking meat *ispod peke* – under a cast-iron bell surrounded by hot ashes, so the food cooks slowly and all the juices are retained. This iron bell is also used to make the Dubrovnik stew known as *zelena menestra*, a hearty dish of slow-cooked smoked ham, sausages, cabbage and potatoes.

Vegetables

Vegetarians are not too well catered for, although the salads are usually fresh and ample; salad with feta cheese (*sirom*) is especially popular, and pasta with a non-meat, tomato-based sauce is usually available. Fresh vegetables (*svježe povrće*) are seasonal (which shows they are both fresh and local), and may include courgettes, aubergines and the ubiquitous Swiss chard (*blitve*). Polenta is a common accompaniment to dishes. You can often get crêpes (*palačinke*), either savoury or sweet. And, of course, there is always pizza, which is usually very good indeed and often comes in eye-poppingly generous portions. But if you want some innovative dishes, try the Old Town's only exclusively vegetarian restaurant, Nishta (see page 96), located just north of Stradun.

Pasta and risotto

Pasta is ubiquitous on menus, many dishes resembling Italian ones on the other side of the Adriatic. Plates of tagliatelle and spaghetti will have the usual tomato-based sauces, but many will also have seafood such as prawns and scampi. And then there's the Istrian flavour of truffle sauces added to noodles. Risotto (*rižot* or *rižoto*) is just as common: *rižot plodovi mora* is a mixed seafood risotto, and *crni rižoto* (black risotto) is made with squid, the rice blackened by the ink.

Cheeses

Influences from northern Croatia can be found here, including Istrian cow's

---

Sweet treats

Peer into the windows of pastry and souvenir shops and you'll see a selection of Dubrovnik delicacies prettily wrapped up. A favourite is *arancini*, which has nothing to do with the Sicilian rice-ball snack but is instead candied orange peel. It's often sold with bags of caramelised almonds (*bruštulane mjendule*), which are offered as nibbles in bars. You'll also see *kotonjata* and *mantala*, which sometimes resemble Turkish delight. The former are cubes of quince (often translated as quince cheese, although there's nothing cheesy about it) and the latter are made from grape must. *Kotonjata* is also poured into moulds to make desserts.

Table with a view

milk cheese infused with truffles and the hard sheep's milk cheese from Pag known as *paški sir*. Dubrovnik has its own version of the latter, which is made into small rounds and preserved in olive oil.

Sweets

Although Croatians have a sweet tooth, judging by the extremely sticky, creamy cakes on sale in pastry shops (*slastičarnice*) and cafés, these are eaten as snacks, usually with coffee. Local people don't go in for puddings in a big way. You are most likely to be offered ice cream (*sladoled*), fresh fruit (*voće*), baklava and *dubrovačka rožata*, the local version of crème caramel, which can be excellent.

THE MENU

Lunch (*ručak*) and dinner (*večera*) will generally have the same menu. Cold starters usually include a Dalmatian platter with *pršut* (like prosciutto), cheese and olives, as well as soups, octopus salad and marinated anchovies. Warm starters include pasta and risotto dishes, most of which are big enough to suffice as a main course. Grilled meats, skewered fish and seafood platters are common main courses, as are whole grilled fish. As fresh fish is often charged by the kilo, agree the price beforehand to save any unpleasant surprises when it comes to paying the bill.

WHERE TO EAT

Al fresco dining dominates, adding a relaxed sense of informality even during chillier months when heaters are brought outside. Even the restaurants in the Old Town that are tucked away in narrow streets usually find space to plant tables outside. High-end restaurants in historic locations, such as Restaurant 360° (closed in winter) above the Old Port, will have prices to match. Prijeko in the Old Town, which runs parallel to Stradun, is one long street of restaurants, but most are of very average quality. A few honourable exceptions include Stara Loza (see page 98), Wanda (see page 98) and the vegetarian restaurant Nishta (see page 96).

SNACKS

A typical bakery (*pekara*) will have savoury filo pastry pies and sweet pastries, with the latter more prevalent in pastry shops (*slastičarnice*). If you want a second breakfast, the Dubrovnik version of brunch is *marenda*, which consists of usually smaller and cheaper versions of lunch dishes. Ribar in the Old Town does a good selection of *tople* (warm) *marende* including stuffed cabbage leaves (*sarma*) and *šporki makaruli*, a meat pasta dish that is traditionally served on St Blaise's day.

Little hole-in-the-wall pizza takeaways will sell pizza by the slice. Wine

Korčula is known for its white wines

bars in the Old Town often serve plates of cheese and charcuterie to go with your wine, which make an appetising aperitif or even a meal in itself.

MEALS

Restaurant is *restoran*, but many eating places describe themselves as a *konoba*, which was originally a kind of rustic tavern. It still is in some rural areas, but in the city the meaning has become blurred. Some upmarket restaurants cheerfully call themselves a *konoba*, while a humbler establishment is a *restoran*. Many cafés (often spelled *caffe* the Italian way) have full menus for lunch and dinner as well.

DRINKS

The vineyards in the Pelješac peninsula just north of Dubrovnik are home to some of Croatia's top wines, but as they're rarely exported they might not be familiar to the average wine drinker. Red wine (*crno vino*) prevails in this part of the Dalmatian coast, the primary grape of which is *plavac mali*. This produces one of the best wines in the region, the full-bodied *Dingač*. *Postup* is a darker red from the same grape. White wines (*bijelo vino*) include *pošip*, grown on the island of Korčula, and *dubrovačka malvasija*.

The local dessert wine is *prošek*, which gained notoriety when Croatia joined the European Union in 2013.

EU officials assumed there would be confusion between this sweet dessert wine and prosecco, a dry sparkling wine from Italy, and ordered the Croatian producers to change the name that had been in existence for about 2,000 years. Not surprisingly, Croatia launched an appeal.

The Croatian national spirit, *rakija*, is made from distilled alcohol flavoured with fruit or herbs. There's also a version made from walnuts called *orahovac*. The recipes for it differ not only from place to place but also from distiller to distiller.

Many people drink beer (*pivo*) with meals. Croatian beer is tasty, inexpensive and not too high in alcohol. Dubrovnik's water (*voda*) is safe to drink and tastes fine, and most restaurants will offer carafes of tap water free of charge, although they are more than happy to sell you bottled mineral water if that is what you want. Coffee (*kava*) is usually strong and good. Coffee with milk is *kava s mlijekom*; if you want it black, ask for *kava* or espresso.

Food and Drink Prices

Approximate prices are based on a two-course meal for one, with a bottle of house wine.
€ = under 300 kn
€€ = 300–500 kn
€€€ = over 500 kn

Croatia claims to be the original home of the tie

SHOPPING

Although Dubrovnik is not the place for serious shopping, there's a growing number of independent Croatian boutiques and designers to be found among the souvenir shops. And there's certainly no shortage of places to buy high-quality food.

Dubrovnik doesn't have the range of shops you would expect of such a heavily visited city, but there are few local items worth looking out for.

MARKETS

Dubrovnik's markets are the best places to browse and to buy fresh local produce – useful not only for those in self-catering accommodation but for putting together a picnic or simply buying whatever is in season.

The main markets are the daily ones in Gruž Harbour – where there is also a big, noisy fish market – and in Gundulić Square in the Old Town. The former is an authentically local affair, worth visiting if you can get there early, because this is when Gruž really comes to life. It's very convenient if you are about to get on a morning ferry and haven't had time for breakfast.

The Gundulić Square market also specialises in fresh produce but, being in the heart of tourist territory, has goods geared towards foreign visitors as well. You will find embroidered linen and lace, and products derived from locally grown lavender: bottles of oil, attractively wrapped soaps and pretty linen lavender bags. You will also see local honey for sale here, strings of fresh garlic, bags of nuts and little coronets of dried figs, garlanded with leaves.

JEWELLERY

Silver filigree is the speciality, and coral also features frequently. Dubrovnik Treasures (www.dubrovniktreasures.com) at Celestina Medovića beside the Franciscan Monastery makes by hand original designs and will also make jewellery to your specifications at reasonable prices. Modni Kantun at Zlatarska 3 stocks beautifully crafted accessories made by Croatian artisans.

FASHION

Although the choice is not extensive, you can find contemporary fashion in Dubrovnik. Je*s, in Od Puča 7, is the place for trendy high-street labels such as Desigual. There's another branch in the Robna Kuća Minčeta (www.minceta.hr) shopping centre near Gruž harbour, which also has a decent number of men's and women's shops. For upmar-

Lace is a popular souvenir

ket fashion, MaxMara has a branch in Gundulić Square. The biggest selection of designer clothes in one space is in Maria Boutique (www.mariastore.hr) near the Ploče Gate, featuring several dozen names including Stella McCartney and Marni.

WINE AND FOOD

A wide range of wines and local spirits can be found in supermarkets – some in attractive bottles, which make nice gifts. For more upmarket choices, try Vinoteka, a well-stocked wine shop with helpful service on the corner of Od Sigurate and Stradun. Dubrovačka Kuća in Sveti Dominika sells wine, *rakija* (brandy) and oil, and good-quality but fairly expensive souvenirs. These include embroidered cushion covers and strings of Licitar hearts – honey cakes that are dried, painted red and decorated.

TIES AND HATS

Ties, they say, were invented in Croatia. In the mid-17th century the cravat, a loosely tied scarf worn by Croatian soldiers, became popular in Paris when it was seen adorning the necks of Croatian mercenaries in the service of Louis XIII. A range of high-quality pure silk ties, made by the Potomac Company, can be found in Boutique Croata at Pred Dvorom 2 (near the Cathedral) and in the same company's outlet in the Hotel Excelsior.

Even if you never wear a hat, Ronchi, at Lučarica 2, just off Luža Square, is worth a visit. They have been making hats since 1858 and display some wonderful creations.

EMBROIDERY AND LACE

You will not have to look far for these items. In fact they are hard to avoid. In the large square just outside Pile Gate, stalls offer all kinds of embroidered linen and lace, along with handmade dolls and other trinkets. In the Old Port, women sit crocheting and embroidering the goods spread out for sale: tablecloths, napkins, cushion covers, handkerchiefs and baby clothes. More of the same can be found under the archway between Luža Square and the port, and on the steps leading to the Dominican Monastery.

PAINTINGS AND PRINTS

A number of small shops and galleries sell work by contemporary Croatian artists, usually at reasonable prices. In Sveti Dominika you will find interesting works in the Sebastian Art Gallery (in the old St Sebastian church). In Marojice Kabog (running between Stradun and Od Puča), the Atelier Romana Milutin-Fabris (www.romana-milutin.com) concentrates on the work of this Dubrovnik-born artist. In Lučarica, the next street along, towards St Blaise's Church, the Artur Galerija (www.arturgallery.com) is also worth a look.

Folk dancers in full swing

ENTERTAINMENT

With a few exceptions, Dubrovnik isn't known for its throbbing nightlife. Its scene is centred more on its lively cafés and bars – but it's a very different story during the Summer Festival when revellers fill the streets.

CLASSICAL MUSIC

Throughout the summer, classical concerts are held in a number of different venues. The Dubrovnik String Quartet and the Sorkočević Quartet give recitals in St Saviour's Church beside the Franciscan Monastery. The Dubrovnik Symphony Orchestra performs in the city's historic venues such as the Dominican Monastery, the Revelin Fortress and the Rector's Palace. Flaming torches are placed outside the venue where an event is being held.

FOLK MUSIC

The Linđo Folklore Ensemble, highly esteemed throughout Croatia, performs folk dance and song on an outdoor stage in the Lazareti on summer evenings. There are also folk dance performances on Sunday morning in Luža Square and in the village of Čilipi (near the airport).

NIGHTLIFE

Head to the Ploče Gate and beyond for a trio of venues offering contrasting nights out. Culture Club Revelin (www.clubrevelin.com) attracts international DJs to its two floors of club space, plus a huge terrace. Just outside the gate is Lazareti (www.lazareti.com), which puts on a more cutting-edge programme of electronica and punk within the buildings of the old quarantine houses. Next to that is Banje Beach Nightclub (www.banjebeach.com), a classic beach club that keeps going till 4am.

In the Old Town, the focus is on bars and cafés, including La Bodega near the Sponza Palace, D'Vino Wine Bar in Palmotićeva near the Franciscan Monastery and the cafés encircling Gundulić Square. There are a few "Irish" pubs – notably Karaka (www.irishpubkaraka.com) and Gaffe – which get busy during big sporting events, but don't assume there's anything remotely Irish about them. Jazz Caffe Troubadour lives up to its name with live jazz playing most nights in the summer.

Outside the Pile Gate, Sky Bar draws a young crowd to its downstairs dance floor (don't be fooled by the name), and further along Branitelja Dubrovnik is the much cooler Art Café.

Trendy Banje Beach club

Off the tourist trail but popular among locals is the string of bars and cafés on Ulica Iva Vojnovića in Lapad, especially Culto and Mirakul.

One of the fastest-growing events in Dubrovnik is Orsuladanja, a series of live concerts staged in July and August at Park Orsula, a large amphitheatre clinging to the hillsides just south of the city. It's an incomparable setting to watch the sun set over Dubrovnik's Old Port to a soundtrack of music from mainly regional bands. It's a five-minute drive from the city, or you can take the half-hour walk along an ancient path through the woods.

FESTIVALS

There are two major festivals in Dubrovnik: the celebrations for St Blaise's day in early February, and the Summer Festival in July and August.

Annual events

St Blaise's day is 3 February. The festival is ceremonially opened the preceding afternoon outside St Blaise's church, and at 10am on the day a celebratory Mass is held in front of the Cathedral, followed by a procession. The town is decked with flags and banners and the whole population joins in. The ceremony culminates in the bishop blessing them all before releasing three white doves. Festivities continue throughout the day with music, dancing and lots of food.

February is also the month for the pre-Lenten carnival, with colourful parades in Stradun and masked balls in the large hotels. Processions are also held in Cavtat.

Dubrovnik's Summer Festival, inaugurated in 1950, lasts for about six weeks from early July to late August. It is a wonderful time to be in the city, but you need to book accommodation well in advance or you will have little chance of finding a room.

Performances are staged all over the city and usually include a performance of *Hamlet* in the dramatic setting of Fort Lovrijenac. The Marin Držić theatre puts on dramatic and musical performances, including a number by Držić himself, the city's favourite 16th-century playwright. Numerous concerts are held in the beautiful atrium of the Rector's Palace. Then there are the streets of the Old Town itself, where the Natural Theatre Company performs, music is played, flaming torches burn and costumed figures add to the atmosphere.

Other annual events include the Dubrovnik Film Festival in late October and Cavtat's Summer Festival in July and August, with music and water polo tournaments. On 29 July, St Theodor's Day in Korčula is celebrated with the Moreška Sword Dance Festival. This colourful ritual – essentially a mock battle between good and evil – draws large crowds as brass bands play the battle march.

Kayaking near the City Walls

OUTDOOR ACTIVITIES

This part of the Adriatic coast has many ways to tempt outdoorsy types as well as swimmers keen to explore the clear blue waters. Learn to dive or take to the hills on a hike or bike ride.

Although Dubrovnik is principally a city destination, there are a number of sports and outdoor activities on offer. Most are on the water, but other activities take advantage of the rugged and dramatic landscapes throughout the region.

SWIMMING

Dubrovnik's main beach, Banje, is a pebbly one just beyond the Ploče Gate, where you can also water-ski. It's mainly public although part of it is sectioned off for one of the beach bars. About 1.5km (0.9 miles) further south is a stretch of shingle, pebbles and a little sand at Sveti Jakov past the Villa Dubrovnik hotel. West of the old town is a rocky beach at the Danče promontory. Other rocky beaches are accessible from the Buža Bar beneath the City Walls.

The pebbly beach in Lapad Bay has a full range of facilities for families, as does the large pebbly Copacabana beach on the Babin Kuk peninsula. Copacabana also has facilities for disabled people.

Take the little ferry to Lokrum and choose from the shallow saltwater lake and the rocky and shingle beaches on the southern side where's there also a naturist beach.

Your best bet for sandy beaches would be to head to Šunj on Lopud and Saplunara beach on Mljet.

DIVING

The vibrant, colourful underwater world of this southern part of the Adriatic can be explored on diving trips with Blue Planet (tel: 091-899 0973; www.blue-planet-diving.com), based at the Hotel Dubrovnik Palace in Lapad. You can choose from beginner PADI courses to half-day, full-day and night dives among shipwrecks and in subterranean caves.

BOATING

Sea kayaking, rafting and canoeing are popular and easy to arrange. Sea kayaking in the bay between Fort Bokar and Fort Lovrijenac (just outside the City Walls) is run by Adventure Dalmatia (tel: 091-526 3813, www.adventure dalmatia.com). Kayaking around Lokrum Island (with transfers from the city) is organised by Adria Avanture (tel: 020-311 545; www.adriaadventure.hr) and Adriatic Kayak Tours (tel: 020-312 770; www.adriatickayaktours.com), which also

Korčula yachts   *Wreck diving*

offers kayaking from Lopud to Šipan and cycling around Šipan.

Get a taste of sailing by renting a sailboat with a skipper who can give you a personalised tour of the waters around Dubrovnik and the islands. Adventure Dubrovnik (tel: 099-336 1336; www.adventuredubrovnik.com) has three-hour tours on small boats, and also gives you the opportunity to become a temporary member of the crew of a racing yacht.

CYCLING

Cycling is becoming more popular in the region, particularly along the Konavle coast starting at Cavtat. You can hire a bike at Teuta at Trumbićev put 3 in Cavtat (020-479 786; www.cavtat.biz) and explore some of the varied trails along the coast. Part of the daily hire includes a transfer to one of the uphill routes.

If you take a day trip to Mljet, hire a bicycle at Polače harbour to make the most of the wooded trails winding through the island's national park.

WALKING

Rather than take the cable car, join a guided walk up to Mount Srđ with Adventure Dalmatia (tel: 091-526 3813, www.adventuredalmatia.com), which includes a visit to the Museum of the Homeland War. Adventure Dubrovnik (tel: 099-336 1336; www.adventuredubrovnik.com) runs a similar excursion which is timed to catch the sunset over the city.

Lapad and Babin Kuk have a network of footpaths that cover most of the peninsula and run along the coast.

The Ronald Brown walking trail in Cavtat is a steep uphill path that rewards you with sweeping views of the bay.

RUNNING

The Dubrovnik international half-marathon takes place in late April/early May and includes a 2km (1.2 miles) dash around the City Walls. Check other running events at www.du-motion.com.

FISHING

Fishermen of any level can join a big-game fishing expedition to catch bluefin tuna, amberjack and swordfish. Big Game Fishing (tel: 091-419 1450; www.biggamedubrovnik.com) runs half-day and day-long excursions.

OTHER ACTIVITIES

Companies such as Konavle Safari in Cavtat (tel: 098 345 526; http://konavlesafari.hr) offer 4-hour Jeep safaris through the countryside of the Konavle region. This is also the site of a biking and wine tasting excursion offered by Adventure Dalmatia (tel: 091-526 3813, www.adventuredalmatia.com), which takes in views of the Konavle valley and its villages. Adventure Dalmatia also gives you the thrilling chance to abseil down Dubrovnik's City Walls and on to Stradun.

Example of Glagolitic alphabet

HISTORY: KEY DATES

From its 7th-century foundation by the Illyrians, through to the Republic of Ragusa, when it was ruled by Venetians, Hungarians and Ottomans, to the 20th-century conflicts and its present status as part of an independent Croatia member of the EU.

EARLY TIMES

4th century BC	Greeks and Illyrians are resident on the coast of Dalmatia.
1st century BC	Romans usurp the earlier settlers and establish the colony of Illiricum.
395	After the division of the Roman Empire, Southern Dalmatia comes under the rule of the western half, until its 5th-century collapse.
555	Dalmatia is conquered by Byzantine Emperor Justinian.
9th century	Cyril and Methodius, 'the apostles of the southern Slavs', convert the masses to Christianity. Cyril invents the Glagolitic alphabet to translate the Bible into the Slavonic language. St Blaise (Sveti Vlaho) becomes patron saint of the city.

FOREIGN RULE

999	Venetians capture Croatian coast for the first time.
12th century	Settlements of Ragusa and Dubrovnik united when Stradun is paved over.
1181	First recorded mention of the Republic of Ragusa.
1202	Fourth Crusade. The Venetians demand the submission of Dubrovnik and install a Venetian as rector.
1358	Under the Peace of Zadar, Hungary gains control of Dubrovnik.
1433	Council of Basel gives papal permission for Dubrovnik to trade with Muslim countries.
1560	Jesuits arrive in Dubrovnik.
15–16th centuries	Dubrovnik School of painting flourishes.
1667	Earthquake destroys much of Dubrovnik. Many great works of art are lost.
1806	Napoleon occupies the city. Two years later he dissolves the Republic.

Siege of Dubrovnik, 1991

NATIONAL REVIVAL

Mid-19th century	Romantic Nationalist Illyrian movement seeks the unification of Southern Slavs.
1905	Stjepan Radić forms the Croatian Peasants' Party.
1919	Under the Versailles Peace Treaty the Kingdom of Serbs, Croats and Slovenes comes into being, with King Aleksander at its head.
1928	Radić assassinated by a Serb MP.
1929	Aleksander forms a dictatorship, calls it the Kingdom of Yugoslavia.
1934	Aleksander assassinated by members of the Ustase Croatian fascist movement.

WORLD WAR II TO THE PRESENT DAY

1941	Axis powers invade Yugoslavia and install the Ustase in power.
1944	Tito enters Belgrade at head of Red Amy, backed by Allied powers.
1945	Socialist Republic of Yugoslavia comes into being.
1953	Tito elected president. Initiates Non-Aligned Movement and decentralises the economy.
1960s	Tourist industry flourishes.
1980	Death of Tito.
1979	Dubrovnik declared a Unesco World Heritage Site.
1990	Franjo Tudjman elected president, at the head of the Croatian Democratic Union (HDZ).
1991	Break-up of Federal Republic.
1991–92	Homeland War. Dubrovnik besieged.
1990s	Rebuilding of damaged city goes ahead; tourist industry flourishes.
1999	Death of Tudjman.
2003	HDZ returns to power under more moderate president Stjepan Mesić and prime minister Ivo Sanader. Croatia applies for EU membership.
2009	Croatia joins NATO.
2012	Sanader convicted of corruption charges.
2013	Croatia joins the European Union on 1 July.
2015	Kolinda Grabar-Kitarović of the centre-right HDZ party becomes the first female president in the post-independence era.
2017	Dubrovnik's newly elected mayor Mato Franković (HDZ) enforces a cap on the number of tourists visiting the Old Town.

BEST ROUTES

Peeking through the City Walls

AROUND THE CITY WALLS

One of the best ways to start a visit to Dubrovnik is by taking a walk around the City Walls to get a feeling for the layout and the history of the city. This route also includes Fort Lovrijenac and Danče church, just outside the walls.

DISTANCE: 2km (1.2 miles)
TIME: A full day
START: Outside the Pile Gate
END: Pile Gate
POINTS TO NOTE: If you're staying in Lapud, Babin Kuk or Gruž, you can take bus No 4, 5 or 6 to reach the Pile Gate. Start as early as you can to avoid the midday heat and the tour group crowds. Remember a hat and sunblock, but you can get refreshments on the way round although you'll end up paying a premium for them. Entrance is payable only in kuna and by credit card; no euros are accepted. Don't leave the walls until you have finished your walk as you will have to pay another entrance fee if you wish to return.

There is usually a bit of a scrum outside the **Pile Gate ❶** as passengers are disgorged from tour group buses. Above it all, a figure of Sveti Vlaho (St Blaise), the city's patron, holding a model of Dubrovnik, looks down with a benign expression. Through the gate and down a few steps is the inner gate, and immediately to the left, inside the fortifications, is one of the three entrances to the **City Walls** (open 8am–6.30pm or 7.30pm Apr– Sept, till 5.30pm in Oct, 9am–3pm Nov–Mar; charge, which also gives admission to Fort Lovrijenac).

WESTERN VIEWS

As you climb the long flight of stone steps you can catch sight of the roofs and cloister of the **Franciscan Monastery ❷** (see route 2) before turning left. The route is a one-way system that goes anti-clockwise around the walls. **Fort Lovrijenac** looms ahead to your right on the headland across the bay.

To your left you can a glimpse of the everyday life of Dubrovnik, with narrow houses, carefully tended, flower-filled gardens and children playing ball. The shiny newness of some of the terracotta roof tiles shows which ones were shattered by shell and mortar fire in 1991, and you can also spot ruins from the 1979 earthquake. Soon you

Sea view from the walls

see the circular **Bokar Fortress** ❸, designed in the 15th century by Italian architect Michelozzo Michelozzi, jutting out into the sea. As you veer to the left there's the first refreshment stop, a tiny kiosk that sells cold drinks.

South side of the city

Here the island of Lokrum slides into view on your right. Some of the houses beyond the walls are so close that you can peer into their windows, but you might want to resist the temptation. Before you reach the next fortress, **Sveti Margarita** ❹, you can catch views of the chapel to the rear of St Mary's Convent and the Jesuit Church among the neat vegetable gardens.

At the fortress there's a small souvenir shop and café with tables set outside if you want to stop for a drink. Ahead you'll see pinned to the outer wall of the next fortress, **Sveti Stjepan** ❺, a figure of St Blaise, and perhaps wonder how he was manoeuvred and fixed in this seemingly precarious position.

As you approach **Sveti Spasitelj Fortress** ❻ you'll see **Caffe Bar Salvatore** (see ❶), which teems with visitors enjoying the shade of the café umbrellas in the height of the season. Just as popular are the public toilets here, which are the only free public ones in the old town.

MARITIME MUSEUM

Arriving on the western side of the walls, you see Sveti Ivan Fortress, which was built in the 14th century and now houses the **Maritime Museum** ❼ (Pomorski Musej; open Tues–Sun 9am–10pm winter 9am–4pm; http://dumus.hr/en/maritime-museum). Laid out over two spacious floors, the air-conditioned museum gives an interesting glimpse into the history of this maritime city. There are models of 16th-century carracks and galleons, an illuminated view of the port before the Great Earthquake of 1667 (the original painting is in the Franciscan Monastery collection), pictures of 19th- and early 20th-century steamships and their masters, and photographs of boats burning in the harbour during the 1991–92 siege.

City Walls tips

This is one of the most popular attractions in Dubrovnik, so be prepared for slow-moving crowds of visitors if you go in high season. To make an attempt at evading the worst of the crowds, be prepared to start the walk the minute the ticket office opens at 8am, as the cruise-ship visitors will descend shortly after that. The paths can be quite narrow and the walls are relatively low; this could be a problem if you have difficulty with heights. Most importantly, wear sturdy flat shoes to cope with the numerous stone staircases throughout the walk.

City Wall shadows

THE HARBOUR

Follow the walls now above the harbour, busy with the traffic of small craft coming and going to Cavtat and Lokrum. To your left, you look down on the rear of the ancient churches of St Nicholas and St Sebastian, before

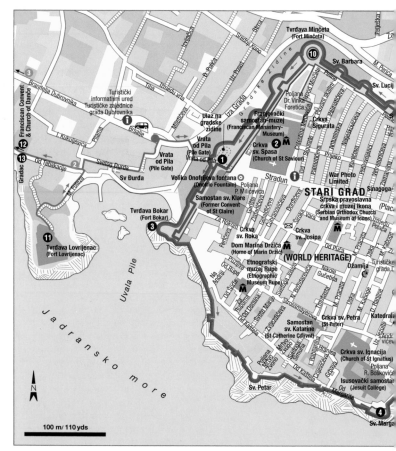

City rooftops, old and new   _The view towards the Old Port_

reaching the **Ploče Gate** entrance, which is one of the three entrances to the walls. After you've finished your walk, you can come back to the gate

[Map showing city walls with labels:]

Srd
Kralja Petra Krešimira IV
Uspinjača (Dubrovnik Cable Car)
Cavtatska
Chodska
Put od Bosanke
Uz Tabor
Hvarska
Dominikanski samostan-muzej (Dominican Monastery-Museum)
Asimon Tower
Tvrđava Revelin (Fort Revelin)
Frana Supila
bratovština
Crkviča Navještenje i sv. Luke
Vrata od Ploča (Ploče Gate)
Trg oružja
va sv. kole
Sv. Dominika
Crkva sv. Sebastijana (St Sebastian Church)
Sv. Luka
y stup (olumn) ck Tower
Sponza-Povijesni arhiv (Sponza Palace - Historic Archives)
Old Port
Stara Luka
Kaše
Mala Onofrijeva fontana (Small Onofrio Fountain)
Kazalište Marina Držića (Martin Držić Theatre)
Lokrum, Cavtat
Knežev dvor (Rector's Palace)
cki
Galerija Dulčić-Masle-Pulitika
Tvrđava sv. Ivana (St John Fortress)
Pomorski muzej (Maritime Museum)
Ponta
minska a muzej
Kneza Damjana Jude
Akvarij (Aquarium)
Porporela
na ića
Od Pustijerne
Dura Baljev
Braće Andrijća
Stjepa Za Kamenom
Crkva Gospe od Karmena (Our Lady of Carmen)
Porporela
Restićeva
Ispod Mira
Sv. Spasitelj
Sv. Stjepan

and check out the colourful displays of handmade lace products laid out at the bottom of the steps.

As you round a bend in the walls, your views out to sea are over the Revelin Fortress, the Lazareti and the coast stretching down towards Cavtat. You also get a bird's-eye view of the 360° restaurant terrace at Revelin.

Below are the rooftops of the Dominican Monastery and its Gothic-Renaissance bell tower. Begun in 1390, this tower, with its two great bells, dominates the city, although it faces stiff competition from the Cathedral's lantern dome and the great bulk of the Jesuit Church.

To your left is the upper entrance to the **Dulčić, Masle, Pulitika Gallery ❽** (Tue–Sun 9am–3pm; www. ugdubrovnik.hr), which showcases works by Croatian artists Ivo Dulčić, Antun Masle and Đuro Pulitika. It's also the location of the Ronald Brown Memorial House.

NORTHERN VIEWS

The next fortress, **Sveti Jakova ❾**, is the third entrance to the City Walls. As you continue along the north side of the city, all the views are breathtaking, and you will have to squeeze your way through the crowds if you're there in high season. This is the classic panorama of Dubrovnik's terracotta rooftops, with Lokrum in the background.

Pile Gate provides the most dramatic entrance to the Old Town

Soon you reach the highest point on the walls, the **Minčeta Fortress** ❿, designed and built, like the Rector's Palace, by Michelozzo Michelozzi and Dalmatian Juraj Dalmatinac. By this point in the tour, you will have walked up and down numerous steps, but this final climb to the top of the tower is worth it for the views.

As you descend, you get a closer peek into the cloister of the Franciscan Monastery before you reach street level and the end of the circuit.

FORT LOVRIJENAC

This walk will probably have taken you 1.5 to 2 hours, so you might want a cool drink before you go any further. Refill your bottle with the clean and refreshing water that gushes out of the **Onofrio fountain** in front of the City Walls ticket office. The next stage of the route takes you out of the Pile Gate and down Svetoga Đurđa, the narrow alley beside Brsalje square. You reach a tiny chapel (Sv. Đurđa) at one side of Brsale bay, where there's a little fishing jetty. The **Orhan Restaurant** (see ❷) sits on the other side of the bay, at the foot of 165 steps that must be climbed to reach **Fort Lovrijenac** ⓫ (same hours as the City Walls). Above the entrance to the fortress an inscription reads 'Non Bene Pro Toto Libertas Venditur Auro' (Freedom should not be sold for all the treasure in the world). This mas-

sive, early 16th-century structure was regarded as vital to the defence of the city, and its commander, like the Republic's rectors was changed on a monthly basis to prevent an opportunist from gaining a power base and staging a coup. The leaders of the Ragusan Republic, it seems, were cautious to the point of paranoia. The fort features in the ever-popular Game of Thrones series and is the venue for performances of *Hamlet* during the Summer Festival (July–Aug; www.dubrovnik-festival.hr). A more dramatic setting for the tragedy would be hard to imagine.

DANČE CHURCH

Back down the many steps now for a well-deserved lunch on the vine-clad terrace of the Orhan Restaurant. If you come at the weekend, it's advisable to book in advance. Afterwards, follow the narrow road called Od Tabakarije through a pretty little neighbourhood and up a hill. Ahead of you, where the roads Frana Bulića and Dante Alighieri meet, stands an imposing building belonging to the Dubrovnik University. Turn left and follow the road through a car park atop a headland, then down a pine-shaded slope where the air is scented with herbs.

You will soon reach the **Franciscan Convent and Church of Dance** ⓬, built on the site of a medieval leper colony. There is a well-tended gar-

The impressive fortifications

den here and a little cemetery. The convent is still a functioning one and there are usually nuns around who will let you into the church, but this cannot be guaranteed. The main reason to come here is to see the Lovro Dobričević polyptych (1465) above the altar, one of only three of this artist's works to have survived. Respect the nuns' silent prayer and meditation, and remember to drop a little something in the donations box to the right of the door before you leave. If for any reajson you can't gain access to the church, your journey will not have been wasted, because it is a peaceful and beautiful spot, filled with the sound of birdsong.

JOURNEY'S END

From here, you could follow the example of many local people and take the path down to the cove below, a popular swimming spot. Or you can go back up to the car park and turn left, to find yourself in a shady and usually empty park – **Gradac** ⓭ – where there is a small fish pond and fountain, benches set beneath the trees, and far-reaching views out to sea. From the park, follow Frana Bulića back to the university and take the right-hand fork down Dante Alighieri. (The poet's bust sits on a plinth at the far end.) If you want a funky place to stop for coffee or a cocktail, turn left on to the busy Branitelja Dubrovnika to the **Art Café**

(see ❸), whose quirky decor features carved-out bathtubs as seats. Afterwards, you can head back to the Pile Gate and the bus stops where this route began.

Food and Drink

❶ CAFFE BAR SALVATORE
Gradska Zidine bb; tel: 0 981 698 062; daily 8am–9pm Apr–Oct; www.dubrovnikoldtownrestaurant.com; €
Once you've accepted the fact that you'll be surrounded by people and will have paid over the odds for a cold drink, relax and bask in gorgeous views of Lokrum from the top of the City Walls.

❷ ORHAN RESTAURANT
Od Tabakarije 1; tel: 020-411 918; www.restaurant-orhan.com; daily 9am–midnight €€–€€€
Hidden away by the water's edge beneath Fort Lovrijenac, Orhan serves excellent fish and seafood indoors or outside on a small, vine-draped terrace. Best to book in high season.

❸ ART CAFÉ
Branitelja Dubrovnika 25; daily 9–2am; €
Slink into a cushion-filled carved-out bathtub and enjoy a coffee, cocktail or smoothie in this lively bar with a sheltered terrace.

STRADUN AND OLD TOWN HIGHLIGHTS

You haven't seen Dubrovnik until you've explored its historic heart of marble and gleaming baroque architecture wedged within the old city walls. And its main artery, Stradun, is simply one of the most beautiful streets in Europe.

DISTANCE: 1km (0.6 miles)
TIME: A full day
START: Outside the Pile Gate
END: Gundulić Square
POINTS TO NOTE: This could be spread out over two days if you want to pace yourself and avoid getting saturated with museums and churches. Most museums close on Monday, but many open every day in summer.

To many, **Stradun** ❶ – also known as Placa – is Dubrovnik, that glistening marble-paved thoroughfare that runs between Pile and Ploče Gates. This route takes a leisurely tour along this main artery and off to the many museums, galleries and squares within the walls of the old town, all of which is pedestrianised.

As you cross Pile Gate's drawbridge and enter through the inner and outer gates, immediately to your right is the domed 15th-century Large Onofrian Fountain. It was named after the Italian engineer Onofrio della Cava, who masterminded Dubrovnik's first mains water supply. Behind the fountain is the huge cloister of St Clare's Convent.

THE FRANCISCAN MONASTERY

On the left-hand side of **Stradun**, by the entrance to the City Walls (see route 1) is the Sveti Spas (Church of Our Saviour), which is often closed in the day but is the venue for chamber music concerts on Sunday, Monday and Wednesday evenings in summer. Next door is the **Franciscan Monastery and Museum** ❷ (Musej Franjevačkog Samostana; open daily Apr–Oct 9am–6pm, Nov–Mar 9am–5pm; see page 30). On your left, inside the main entrance, is a delightful, old – but still functioning – **pharmacy** with ornate shelves and ceramic jars. Then you step into the beautiful Romanesque-Gothic cloister, where capitals on the slender columns are decorated with human and animal figures and floral motifs. These survived the earthquake of 1667, which damaged the monastery and church,

Stradun at dusk

and the 19th-century depredations when French and Austrian troops were barracked here at different times and used the cloister to stable their horses. Frescoes depicting the life of St Francis and his arrival in Dubrovnik decorate the walls; in the centre, where herbs for the original pharmacy used to be grown, a statue of the saint stands on a fountain.

Within the **museum** are some fine paintings, among which a 15th-century polyptych featuring St Blaise, by Lovro Dobričević, stands out. There is also a collection of reliquaries and chalices and some splendid 15th-century illustrated manuscripts. In the pharmacy section, reinstated in its original position, ancient jars, bowls and implements are displayed. The monastery was hit by numerous shells during the 1991–92 siege, and the hole pierced in the wall by one missile shot has been preserved behind glass.

You pass from the monastery into the **church** (open 6.30am–noon, 4–7.30pm; free if entered from the street), where the altars are baroque replacements for those destroyed in the 17th-century earthquake. Above the main one is a fine marble *Christ Resurrected* by Ivan Toschini (c. 1712), and the altar of Anthony of Padua is surrounded by a delightful painting by Ivo Dulčić (1916–75), installed here in 1962. To the left of the main altar a plaque commemorates the revered poet Ivan Gundulić (1589–1638), who is buried here. Best of all, however, is the *Pietà* outside, above the main (south) door – a lovely, soulful piece that managed to

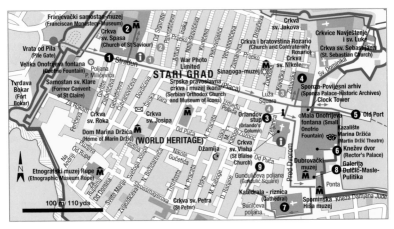

Marble-paved Stradun

survive the earthquake and subsequent fire.

STRADUN AND LUŽA SQUARE

Back in the bustle of Stradun you can stop by the perennially popular **Festival Café** (see ❶). Although Stradun gets crowded when cruise ship groups are being shepherded around, it's a great street to stroll along; you can admire the uniform curved doorways and green shuttered windows of the elegant buildings, and watch reflections dance in the mirror-like surface of the street. There are two good bookshops, a small gallery or two, and a couple of shops selling high-quality clothes as well as plenty of souvenir shops.

The narrow lanes off Stradun are full of inviting bars, tiny restaurants, galleries and shops clinging to the stone steps that eventually lead to Prijeko. If you want a quiet stop for coffee, turn left into Palmotićeva towards **Glam Café** (see ❷). Opposite is D'Vino wine bar (www.dvino.net), one of the city's most convivial places to spend the evening.

Stradun is not a long street, and soon you reach the far end, **Luža Square**, where **Orlando's Column** ❸ stands in the centre, as it has since 1418. Orlando is also known as Roland, as in the *Chanson de Roland*. The story linking him with the defence of Ragusa in the 9th century is without any foundation whatsoever, and chronologi-

cally impossible, but he has become a much-loved symbol of freedom. Straight ahead of you as you stand at Orlando's feet is the great **Clock Tower**, its bell chimed by the hammers of little green men, and with a rather anachronistic digital clock below. Beneath the clock, to the right, is the **Small Onofrio Fountain**, designed, like the larger one, by della Cava, a pretty little creation, popular with pigeons and as a backdrop for tourists' photographs.

SPONZA PALACE AND ST BLAISE

To the left is a rare survivor of the 1667 earthquake, the **Sponza Palace** ❹ (usually open 9am–9pm, winter until 3pm, sometimes inexplicably closed; free), with the single word Dogana on the metal studded door indicating that this used to be the customs house. This is a beautiful building, the delicate windows Venetian Gothic, the main doorway and upper floor late Renaissance, designed by Pasko Miličević and executed by the Andrijić brothers, the renowned Korčula stonemasons. Inside you can admire a narrow, galleried courtyard, and see the original mechanism from the Clock Tower standing rather forlornly at the end, but leave time to visit the **Memorial Room of the Defenders of Dubrovnik** (open 9am–9pm May–Oct, 10am–3pm Nov–Apr; free) to the left as you go in. Here, photos of those who died in the 1991–92 siege, many of them heartrendingly

Orlando's Column   *The bustling harbour*

young men, are positioned around the walls. Above them are pictures of burning boats and buildings, while a video plays scenes of devastation.

Back in the square the **Church of Sveti Vlaho** (St Blaise) is a baroque structure with an interior that is relatively restrained. As the church of the city's patron it is a favourite place for weddings and baptisms. Within, there's an early 18th-century *Martyrdom of St Blaise* on the organ loft and, on the main altar, a silver statue of Blaise holding a model of the city, which shows what it looked like before the earthquake. The fact that this was the only statue in the church to survive the tremor was taken as evidence of the saint's powers. The stained-glass windows, depicting saints Peter and Paul, Cyril and Methodius, are by Ivo Dulčić (1916–75), one of Dubrovnik's most renowned modern artists.

To the left of the church are the imposing buildings of the **Gradska Vijećnica** (Town Hall), the ornate red-and-gold **Marin Držić Theatre** and the **Gradska Kavana** (Town Café; www.nautikarestaurants.com), within the arches of the old arsenal. With a cavernous interior and broad terraces facing on to the square and the port on the other side, the Gradska Kavana is a Dubrovnik institution. Its building also includes the adjoining Arsenale Restaurant and Wine Bar, and the first-floor Sloboda Cinema (http://kinematografi.org), which shows many Hollywood movies in English, as well as Croatian films.

If you're in the mood for lunch at this point, nip into the penultimate narrow lane on the left before Sponza Palace, Kovačka, for a hearty and inexpensive lunch at **Dundo Maroje** (see ❸).

THE OLD PORT

Walk through the gateway between the Sponza Palace and the Clock Tower to the **Old Port** ❺, where you can take in the glorious views of the harbour and the coastline. It's a bustling place, with restaurants, ice-cream stands, craft stalls and the constant coming and going of small boats shuttling to and from Lokrum.

THE RECTOR'S PALACE

Back in the square, the next on the left is the **Rector's Palace** ❻ (Knežev Dvor; daily 9am–6pm Mar–Oct, 9am–4pm Nov–Feb; www.dumus.hr), home to the Cultural History Museum. The two earlier versions of the palace – the second of which was designed by Onofrio della Cava, who built the fountains – were both destroyed in fairly quick succession in the 15th century by gunpowder explosions in the nearby arsenal, an expensive example of not learning from experience. The current palace, incorporated into the remains by Florentine Michelozzo Michelozzi (1396–1472), has a stunning loggia with intricately

The relics of St Blaise, Dubrovnik's patron saint

carved capitals – both Gothic and Renaissance – atop pillars of Korčula marble. One of the figures on the far right capital is thought to represent Aesculapius, the god of healing. Inside, the atrium, also a harmonious mixture of Gothic and Renaissance, is the venue for Summer Festival events (www.dubrovnik-festival.hr) and for regular concerts by the Dubrovnik Symphony Orchestra (www.dso.hr) throughout the summer. The acoustics are excellent, and it is a magical setting in which to hear music on a summer's night. The bust in the centre commemorates Miho Pracat, the Lopud merchant and mariner who left his entire estate to the Republic and was the only commoner immortalised in this way. (Gundulić, whose statue we shall see shortly, was a nobleman.) Confusingly, the Italian version of Pracat's name – Michaeli Prazotto – is given on the statue.

Visiting the museum, you are directed to the right, through a room containing 16th-century portraits, mostly unattributed, then into the Court Room where there are explanations, in English, about how the court functioned during the Republic. Stairs lead down to a vaulted room where there are excellent portraits of Ivan Gundulić and of mathematician Marin Getaldić (1568–1626), friend and contemporary of Galileo, who conducted experiments in a cave not far from the Ploče Gate. Adjoining this room are the former prison cells, with carved wooden chests and statuary,

including a 15th-century St Blaise from the palace doorway. Back in the atrium, you ascend the wide staircase, where the wooden handrail is supported by huge stone hands, to visit the splendid reconstructed state rooms whose mullioned windows overlook the street and Cathedral. The Republic's rectors, each elected for only one month at a time to prevent them from getting too uppity, were not allowed to leave the palace during their period of office or move their families in with them, but at least they lived in comfort. The Rector's Study (complete with a red-robed model rector) displays a lovely *Baptism of Christ* (1509) by Mihajlo Hamzić.

THE CATHEDRAL

Back in the street, you can't miss the imposing, lantern-domed **Cathedral** ❼ (Apr–Oct Mon–Sat 9am–5pm, Sun from 11am, Nov–Mar Mon–Sat 10am–noon, 3–5pm, Sun 11am–noon, 3–5pm). The original Romanesque building, said to have been financed by Richard the Lionheart after he was shipwrecked on Lokrum, was destroyed in the 1667 earthquake. Its baroque replacement, the work of Italian architects Andrea Buffalini and Paolo Andreotti, completed in 1713, is surprisingly simple, although the side altars are somewhat overblown. Above the severe lines of the modern, marble altar (the earlier one was destroyed in another earthquake in 1979) is a School of Titian polyptych.

The Rector's Palace and Cathedral

The Treasury, to the left of the altar, is tiny, and packed with revered objects. Chief among them are an enamelled gold reliquary of St Blaise's head, and reliquaries in delicate gold and silver filigree of his arms and one leg, which are carried in procession around Dubrovnik on the saint's day, 3 February. Numerous other reliquaries are kept here, as is a copy of Raphael's *Madonna della Seggiola*. (The original is in the Pitti Palace in Florence.) These treasures were first kept in St Stephen's Church, taken to the Revelin Fortress after the 1667 earthquake, then moved to the Dominican Monastery before being brought here on St Blaise's day in 1721.

CONTEMPORARY ART

Opposite the Cathedral, built into the city wall, is the **Dulčić**, **Masle**, **Pulitika Gallery** ❽ (Tues–Sun 9am–3pm; www.ugdubrovnik.hr), a small gallery dedicated to three local artists: Ivo Dulčić (1916–75), whose stained-glass windows you can see in St Blaise's and mosaic altarpiece in the Dominican church; Antun Masle (1919–67), some of whose work is also in the Dominican monastery's collection; and Đuro Pulitika, who lived in Dubrovnik until his death in 2006 at the age of 84, and whose delightfully simple Holy Family hangs in the Dominican church. The collection and the changing exhibitions are small but worth seeing if you are interested in contemporary art. You will prob-

ably notice the influence of these artists on many of the paintings in small private galleries around the town.

The gallery (also accessible from the top of the walls) is housed on the upper floors of the Ronald Brown Memorial House. Brown, the first African-American US Secretary of Commerce, was the leader of an American trade delegation to Croatia whose plane crashed on the mountainside above Cavtat in 1996. You can peep into a room to the left of the entrance, where photographs of Brown and the 34 people who died with him, along with a roll of honour, are displayed, but the door is rarely open.

GUNDULIĆ SQUARE

Go round the back of the Cathedral now, and you will find yourself in Buničeva Poljana, a square full of café tables – and, at night, usually full of noise and music, as it's a popular meeting place. On one corner is the **Jazz Caffe Troubadour**, where live jazz is played most evenings. This square leads into another, larger one, **Gundulićeva Poljana** (Gundulić Square) ❾, named after the 17th-century writer who symbolised Croatian national identity, not only in his own time, but again during the 19th-century nationalist revival and the conflicts of the late 20th century. His statue stands on a plinth in the centre of the square, a handy perch for the resident pigeons who show him no reverence whatsoever.

Gundulić Square really livens up in the evening

Gundulić Square has two separate identities, depending on the time of day you come here. In the morning it is the setting for a lively local market, full of colourful fruit, vegetable and flower stalls, together with a few offering embroidered linen, herbs and lavender. By 1pm, there is scarcely a sign left of this activity, and tables, chairs and sun umbrellas are set out by waiters from a line of restaurants. If you didn't have lunch earlier, this would be a great place for it, or you could return here for an evening meal, when the area is equally lively.

You've reached the end of the itinerary, but if you feel it's time for coffee and cake, go back to **Cele Brunch & Bar** on the corner of Stradun, which does cream cakes (see ❹). If you sit for a while longer, or return here in the evening, you will have a grandstand view of the Croatian version of the Italian *passeggiata* known as the *džir* – strolling up and down the street, stopping to talk to friends, or having a drink or ice cream at a café table while their invariably well-dressed children play ball, ride bikes or chase each other over the shiny paving stones.

Food and Drink

❶ FESTIVAL CAFÉ
Placa bb; tel: 020-321 148; www.cafe festival.com; daily 7.30–2am; €
There's much scope for people-watching in this prime spot by the Pile Gate. It serves food all day, but it's just as good to soak up the atmosphere over a coffee at one of the outdoor tables.

❷ GLAM CAFÉ
Palmotićeva 2; tel: 091-151 8257; daily 9am–midnight; €
This intimate little bar off Stradun is the place for a quiet coffee and a reviving smoothie, where tables squeeze into the narrow stairs going up towards Prijeko. It's a different scene in the evening when people stop by for cocktails.

❸ DUNDO MAROJE
Kovačka bb; tel: 020-321 021; daily 11am–10pm; €
Just off Stradun in a narrow alley by Luža Square is this informal little restaurant serving simply grilled fish and classic seafood pasta and risotto dishes. Meat-eaters aren't left out either with Dalmatian steaks and ćevapčići (meat rissoles) on the menu. It's great value, especially during lunch.

❹ CELE BRUNCH & BAR
Placa 1; tel: 020-423 884; www.cele-dubrovnik.com; daily 11am–10pm; €–€€
You're in the thick of the Stradun action by the Sponza Palace, where tables spill out into Luža Square and live music is played in the evenings. You have the best view for when residents take their evening stroll after the cruise crowds have gone.

In the shadow of the City Walls

AROUND PRIJEKO AND SOUTH OF STRADUN

This leisurely route combines an exploration of the hilly streets north of Stradun with a stroll through the lanes near the southern side of the City Walls. There's also a chance to a swim on a rocky beach.

DISTANCE: 1.5km (0.9 miles)
TIME: Three hours
START: Luža Square
END: Gundulić Square
POINTS TO NOTE: There are opportunities to extend the walk by stopping for a swim, or for a drink with a spectacular sea view. Take a swimming kit if you want to drop into the sea to cool off, and flat shoes are best for the numerous flights of steps that make up the streets north of Stradun.

The streets to the north and south of Stradun are full of character, colour and history. North of Stradun are Prijeko and a series of narrow alleyways with several flights of steps that eventually take you under the shadow of the City Walls. South of Stradun is a warren of little lanes decked with flowers and filled with hole-in-the-wall bars and restaurants. It's a place to get lost and stumble upon unexpected paths and corners.

From Luža Square, go through the archway by the Sponza Palace, past stalls offering embroidered cloths and trinkets, and follow Ulica Sveti Dominika for a few metres. To the right, another arch leads out to the Old Port. Straight ahead is a graceful Gothic staircase leading to the monastery. At the top of the steps, on the right, is the **Sebastian Gallery ①** (open daily 10am–5pm; free), where changing exhibitions of modern art are held (and works sold) in the 15th-century votive church of St Sebastian. Here the cool, white vaulted rooms make an attractive exhibition space. The gallery also sells beautifully hand-crafted jewellery, much of it made from local coral.

THE DOMINICAN MONASTERY

Enter the **Dominican Church and Monastery ②** (Dominikanska Crkva i Samostan; open 9am–6pm, winter until 5pm) through a peaceful cloister, where late-Gothic arcades are embellished with Renaissance motifs. In the centre is a huge well that was last used to supply water for the besieged

The Dominican Monastery

city in 1991–92. Like its Franciscan counterpart, the cloister was used in the 19th century as barracks and stables both by French and Austrian troops.

Among the excellent paintings in the museum are three by Nikola Božidarević (c. 1460–1518): the *Holy Conversation* (1513), showing the *Virgin and Child* with saints and angels; *The Annunciation*, painted some 10 years later; and *The Virgin with*

Saints, in which Mother and Child are flanked by saints Blaise and Paul on one side and Dominic and Augustine on the other. Also look out for Mihajlo Hamzić's triptych, commissioned by the wealthy Lukarević family in 1512, showing an avuncular St Nicholas framed by a Renaissance-style shell. There are also a number of illustrated manuscripts and a collection of reliquaries, including one of the head of St Stephen, first king of Hun-

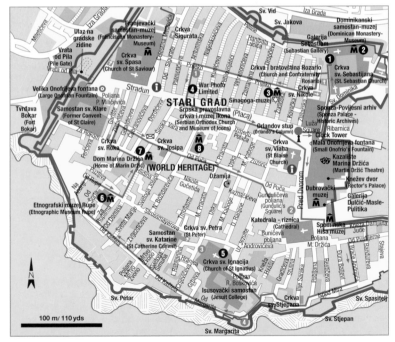

The monastery's cloister   *War Photo Limited*

gary (997–1038). The church, remodelled in baroque style after the 1667 earthquake, has an attractive stone pulpit, and some modern works of art. These include Ivo Dulčić's mosaic altarpiece, Djuro Pulitika's *Holy Family*, a bronze *Virgin and Child* by Ivan Meštrović, and eye-catching stained-glass windows that replaced those that were shattered during the 1991–92 bombardment.

PRIJEKO

The street directly opposite the door of St Sebastian is Prijeko, which runs along to the far end of Stradun and is lined with restaurants – many of average quality. On the right is the Church of the Holy Rosary, on the left the tiny chapel of St Nicholas – both usually closed. Pop down the third street on the left – Žudioska – to visit the **Synagogue and Museum** ❸ (Sinagoga Musej; open May–Oct daily 10am–8pm, Oct–Apr Mon–Fri 10am–3pm). The museum contains parchment Torah scrolls, said to have been brought here by Sephardic Jews after their expulsion from Spain in 1492, as well as embroidered Torah Ark covers, and a list of Dubrovnik's Jewish victims of the Holocaust. On the second floor is a synagogue – small, but more than large enough to accommodate the dozen or so Jewish families that remain in the city.

Back along Prijeko you will be accosted by a flurry of waiters inviting you to sit and eat at one of the tables beneath umbrellas – regardless of the time of day.

IMAGES OF WAR

Further along, look out for Antuninska on the left and you will come to the cosy **Caffe Bar Tinel** (see ❶). A few doors further down is **War Photo Limited** ❹ (May–Sept daily 10am–10pm May and Oct Wed–Mon 10am–4pm; www.warphotoltd.com), an innovative gallery that displays exhibitions of work by award-winning photographers. Exhibitions change regularly, but there are permanent displays of images from the conflicts in the former Yugoslavia. Gallery owner Frederic Hancez, a Belgian businessman, and New Zealand director Wade Goddard, who first came to the region as a war photographer, aim not to shock or sensationalise, but to show the true face of war and remind us that situations remain unresolved when the world's press moves on. The setting, with its high vaulted ceilings, is as dramatic as the images on display.

There are a couple more little streets this side of Stradun to wander up and down before you emerge once more into the town's main artery. Look out for details in the narrow lanes of steep steps: tiny galleries and little shops, hole-in-the-wall cafés where people sit on cushions outside when there's not

The impressive bulk of the Jesuit Church

enough space for even the smallest table and chairs.

SOUTH OF STRADUN

Walk down Stradun towards Ploče and turn right towards the main door of the Cathedral. This district is called Pustjerna, and it's the oldest one in the city. If you're in the mood to amble along, you could nip into some of its arcaded lanes and explore the stony footpaths. But if you're in need of sustenance, stop for a cold drink and some people-watching at **Caffe Bar None Nina** just before the Cathedral (see ❷).

Turn into Ulica Kneza Damjana Jude in front of the Cathedral, where restaurant tables fill the narrow street. Take a right into Bandureva and another right into Braće Andrijića, past the 15th-century Ranjina Palace, a Gothic private residence. The street was named after the Andrijić brothers, who were stonemasons from Korčula, and two streets along, in Restićeva, you will see one of their greatest works, the Renaissance Skočibuha Palace. At the top of Braće Andrijića you come to the foot of the City Walls, where you turn right into Ispod Mira. A short way along, a gateway in the wall leads down a wide rocky path to a concreted bathing area. If you feel like having a swim, this is your chance. Otherwise, continue your walk beneath the walls.

THE JESUIT CHURCH

Briefly leave the shadow of the walls when you see, to your right, the great bulk of the **Jesuit Church** ❺ (Crvka Sveti Ignacija; usually open 7am–8pm; free). Poljana Boškovića, in which it stands, is a slightly untended neighbourhood square with washing hanging outside a few houses and – unlike the church – no pretensions at all. Unless you arrive here when one of the tour groups is visiting, you feel that you could be in a rustic village square, even though you are only about 200 metres/yards from the centre of town. The church was designed by the Jesuit Andrea Pozzo and modelled (inside) on the Gesù Church in Rome. Building work began in 1664, although it was interrupted by the earthquake three years later, and was finally completed in 1725.

You enter through a door flanked by Corinthian columns, to be faced with a massive interior, dominated by marble side altars. The ceiling of the apse, painted by Spanish-Sicilian Gaetano García, shows Ignatius, founder of the Jesuit Order, ascending to heaven amid fluffy white clouds, while the walls are decorated with scenes from his life, and Pozzo's signature trompe l'oeil surrounding them. To the right of the main door is an extremely kitsch Grotto of Lourdes, with a pink-and-white Virgin surrounded by plastic flowers and gazing down on a hopeful pilgrim. At the

Buža Bar's spectacular setting

side of the church is the Jesuit College (Collegium Ragusinum) completed in the 1690s after much controversy. Poet Ivan Gundulić (1589–1638) and mathematician Ruđer Bošković (1711–87), among other prominent Ragusans, were educated here. To the right of the church the Jesuit Steps sweep down towards Gundulić Square.

If you're in the mood to stop for lunch – or plan to return in the evening for an al fresco supper – **Restaurant Kopun** is a good choice (see ❸).

BACK TO THE WALLS

Back under the walls, a sign proclaims 'Cold drinks with the most beautiful view' and a short way along, this is exactly what you get. Pop through a hole in the wall to find **Buža Bar** (see ❹) with tables set on terraces cut into the cliff, stunning sea views and the sight of Lokrum ahead. (Bear in mind that the café will be closed if the weather is bad. Once you see the café, you'll understand why the owners wouldn't risk staying open in high winds and rain.) Carry on along Ulica od Kaštela, and allow yourself to be tempted down any of the little stepped streets to your right, bright with flowery window boxes and flapping washing and with impressive stone balconies and decorated stonework on otherwise humble dwellings. The building you soon pass on the left is the former convent of St Mary, now converted into private apartments.

MUSEUMS IN THE BACK STREETS

After about 100 metres/yards you can follow the walls no longer and must turn down Na Andriji, which takes a sharp turn to the right and deposits you outside the **Rupe Ethnographic Museum** ❻ (Etnografski Musej Rupe; Wed–Mon 9am–10pm, winter until 4pm; http://dumus.hr/en). This 16th-century building was the store house for the government grain reserves, which were kept in the huge dry wells you can still see in the floors. ('Rupe' means hole or cavern.) Upstairs, the museum displays agricultural implements, fishing paraphernalia and ornate festival costumes. The building and the views from the upper windows are of most interest.

A few metres right of the museum (note the wooden ramps over the steps to enable delivery carts to get up here) take the first left, Od Domino, down past the Domino restaurant (www.restaurantdomino-dubrovnik.com) and Domino church. The latter is usually closed during the day but is the venue for concerts on Sunday evening. Next door is the **Home of Marin Držić** ❼ (Dom Marina Držića; open Tue–Sun 9am–10pm, Mon 10am–6pm). Držić (1508–67) is one of Dubrovnik's most revered playwrights, and his works take pride of place in the Summer Festival. In a missed opportunity, however, the museum does not give a great deal of insight into his life. The collection

Gundulić Square

consists of little more than a video about his time in Siena and a rather quirky (free) audio guide in a building that gives only a glimpse into life in the 16th century.

From the museum, go left along Za Rokum and turn right by a small church to reach Od Puča. Historically the street of the silversmiths, busy little Od Puča still has many shops selling gold and silver filigree jewellery, along with souvenir shops, a couple of little galleries, an old-fashioned barber's and a speciality tea and coffee house. On the left is the plain and partially restored Orthodox Church (variable hours) and, next door but one, the **Icon Museum** ❽ (Musej Pravoslavne Crkve; open Mon–Sat 9am–2pm, closed Sat from Nov–Apr). There is an interesting collection within the two rooms, one with Orthodox icons dating from the 15th to 19th centuries, and the other featuring portraits of local Serbs painted by Vlaho Bukovac. It's easy to miss the museum altogether, as the entrance is just inside that of Đardin, an upmarket jewellery shop. If you continue along the street a little further you will find yourself in Gundulić Square, or take any turning on the left and you will be back in Stradun.

Food and Drink

❶ CAFFE BAR TINEL

Antuninska 5; tel: 099-766 3449; €

Stop for a coffee under the vaulted ceiling of this tiny bar, where the walls are covered with arty photos of its customers as well as some original paintings. When the weather is warm, people while away the evening on comfy cushions that line the steps outside.

❷ CAFFE BAR NONE NINA

Pred Dvorom 4; tel: 098-825 844; open 9–2am; €€

At one point or another, most visitors have dropped by None Nina's – only it was called Hemingway and still is by people who can't get used to the new name. It's still one of the best people-watching cafés in the city.

❸ RESTAURANT KOPUN

Poljana Ruđera Boškovića 7; tel: 020-323 969; www.restaurantkopun.com; €–€€

Fresh seafood and Dalmatian meat dishes are served in this romantic restaurant opposite the Jesuit Church. It's especially atmospheric on warm evenings when the outdoor tables spill into the square.

❹ BUŽA BAR

Od Margarite; tel: 095 883 1750; open daily 9am–8pm; €

You might spend a few extra kuna at Buža than you would normally on a drink, but you're sitting at a bar that's been carved into the cliffs, and the view is sublime. As you would expect, it's busy at sunset in summer when it becomes one of the most coveted places for a sundowner.

Harbour view from Ploče Gate

OUTSIDE THE PLOČE GATE

This walk from Ploče Gate leads northeast along a quiet coast road, visiting the Museum of Modern Art and ending at a secluded cove, with an optional trip to Mount Srđ.

DISTANCE: 5km (3 miles)
TIME: Half day
START: Ploče Gate
END: Ploče Gate
POINTS TO NOTE: The walk, with a visit to the museum, can easily be done in two hours, but if you stop for a swim and a drink at one of the beach bars, it could make a satisfying half day out. If you choose to take the cable car to Mount Srđ it will, of course, take more time. There is a longer, more arduous option to hike up Mount Srđ, which is about a 4km (2.5 miles) walk up a zigzagging path and will take more than an hour each way.

In the height of summer, it can be oppressively busy within the City Walls when the cruise ships dock and passengers descend on the Old Town. Escaping the crowds with a stroll along the shore road gives you a different perspective on the city. And a trip up to Mount Srđ rewards you with sweeping views of the coast.

PLOČE GATE AND BANJE BEACH

Outside the **Ploče Gate** ❶, there is a drawbridge and outer and inner gates flanked during the summer months by stoical costumed guards and presided over by St Blaise. On the harbour side is the Revelin Club (www.clubrevelin.com), whose terrace tables offer splendid views and are great for a morning coffee or a sunset drink. On the other side looms the bulk of the **Revelin Fortress** ❷ (open Thur–Tues 10am–4pm), built in the 16th century to protect the town against Turkish attacks from the interior. Its ground floor houses two archaeological exhibits showing medieval church furniture as well as displays showing how the fortress was built. Opposite is a small bar, **Laura** (see ❶), which is a handy spot for a drink before or after the walk.

Out on the main road, Frana Supila, the palatial building on your left is a school, as the sounds emanating from inside will tell you. To the right are the walls of the **Lazareti** ❸ (Frana Supila 8; open Thur–Sat 10pm–5am, winter only Fri and Sat; www.lazareti.com),

Banje Beach, Dubrovnik's recreational shore

which used to be an old quarantine hospital built in the 17th century to keep disease from the city. Its half-dozen buildings now form Dubrovnik's premier arts venue spread over three floors and sprawling towards the beach, with a large courtyard tucked within. Local folklore group Linđo often puts on performances here, and the venue features cinema nights when Croatian and international films are projected on the outside walls. It's also home to a late-night club with appearances by live bands and top DJs from around the world. There are a couple of small galleries at street level, and the cavernous rooms below house textile workshops.

Beside a small post office there are steps leading down to pebbly **Banje Beach 4**, from which you can water-ski. There is another flight of steps further up, near the Hotel Excelsior. Security guards are on duty at either end, but this is a public beach, so you're free to pitch a towel wherever you find a space – or preferably a padded beach mat to protect you from the pebbles. The swish **Banje Beach Club** (www.banje-beach.com) has a cordoned-off section where you can rent canopied loungers if you want a bit of comfort. Because it's the main beach by the Old Town, it gets unbelievably busy in the summer, but the water stays warm until well into the autumn and is a tranquil place out of season.

MUSEUM OF MODERN ART

Past the beach, on the left-hand side at No. 23, is the **Museum of Modern Art 5** (Umjetnička Galerija; Tues–Sun 9am–8pm; http://ugdubrovnik.hr/en). It is housed in a beautiful building that looks pure Renaissance but was actually built in 1935 for a wealthy ship

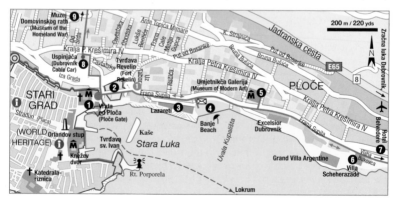

The striking Villa Dubrovnik Hotel

owner. When the doors are closed, it is easy to miss the gallery, as its name is displayed only on a discreet plaque to the left of the entrance. The collection, housed over four floors, with sculptures in the courtyard, is rotated, but invariably includes works by Vlaho Bukovac (1855–1922), who, in 1878, was the first Croatian to be accepted by the Paris Salon. Bukovac was born in Cavtat where more of his work can be seen. Upstairs the collection moves further into the 20th century, and includes works by some of the country's best-known modern sculptors, Ivan Kožarić, Frano Kršnić and Ivan Meštrović. There are also paintings by Ivo Dulčić and Đuro Pulitika, although many of these are now shown in the gallery opposite the Cathedral. On the third floor the palatial salon and terrace threaten to outshine the exhibits, and the top floor is used for changing exhibitions.

FOLLY AND PHILOSOPHY

Almost opposite the gallery is the swanky, recently renovated Hotel Excelsior (www. adriaticluxuryhotels.com), then the interlinked Villa Orsula and Grand Villa Argentina, where the road divides. Take the lower path, Ulica Vlaha Bukovca, where, in lush gardens, stands an Oriental folly known as the **Villa Scheherazade** ❻, built in the early 20th century for a wealthy banking family. All you see from the road, peering through Mozarabic wrought-iron gates, is the shiny tiled blue dome. But you get an excellent view of the folly from the sea on a boat trip to Lokrum, where it looks like something out of a James Bond film. It used to be a privately owned villa, but it was bought by the Adriatic Luxury Hotels group and offers accommodation at a suitably luxurious price.

Next door, but within the gardens, is a tiny chapel with a bell wall and a plaque on the wall informing passers-by that the mathematician and natural philosopher Marin Getaldić (1568–1626) used to conduct experiments in a cave below. (You can see the cave from the sea or when looking back at the end of this walk.) Local people were extremely wary of Getaldić, convinced that his activities in the cave must have had something to do with witchcraft.

Walking along this narrow road, with cypresses and century plants growing on the seaward side and oleanders in gardens on the left, you feel as if you are in a country lane. There's little traffic, particularly after you pass the Villa Dubrovnik Hotel (www.villa-dubrovnik. hr). A short way along you reach the square-towered former monastery of Sveti Jakov (St Jacob), now a private residence, except for the church, which is open only for mass on Sunday. Follow the path as it winds down behind the monastery. There are great views back to town (and to Getaldić's cave) and an unmarked flight of steps down to the lovely sheltered beach of Sveti Jakov, which is mainly pebbly with some sandy sections. During the summer there's a

Stupendous views from the cable car

snack bar and restaurant, and you can rent kayaks, pedalos and jet skis.

NOSTALGIC CORNER

Ahead of you is an old wrought-iron gate on which can just be discerned the words **'Hotel Belvedere'** ❼. Through here, to the left, are the derelict remains of the hotel that suffered so badly in the bombardment of 1991–92. Because it was close to the ridge from which shells and artillery were fired, it stood little chance. A Russian billionaire has bought the ruin to convert it into a luxurious hotel. At present, however, it's an eerie, atmospheric spot, especially out of season.

MOUNT SRĐ AND THE CABLE CAR

Retrace your steps so that you're near the Ploče Gate. On your right you'll see the sign for the **Dubrovnik Cable Car** ❽ (open daily Jun–Aug 9am–midnight, Sep 9am–10pm, Apr and Oct 9am–8pm, Feb, Mar and Nov 9am–5pm, Jan and Dec 9am–4pm; www.dubrovnikcable car.com). Walk along Ulica Iza Grada, turn right on to Zagrebačka and right again on to Kralja Petra Krešimira IV. (If you are taking the Atlas airport transfer bus (www.atlas-croatia.com) back to the airport, this is where you board for the return journey, not at the Pile Gate.)

The 778m (2,552ft) journey up to Mount Srđ takes only a few minutes, but views along the way are wonderful as the car climbs up to the ridge. At the cable car station at the top, there's a souvenir shop and the Panorama restaurant. Outside there's an amphitheatre, which, when it's not being used for weddings, gives visitors ample room to roam around and take in the views of the Elaphite Islands, Lokrum and a wide swathe of the Dalmatian coastline down below. Behind is a stark ridge of bare brown mountains, which contrast dramatically with the blue of the Adriatic Sea.

Your ticket to the cable includes a visit to the **Museum of the Homeland War** ❾ (daily 8am–until sunset; charge if you don't have cable car ticket), which is housed in one wing of the remains of Fort Imperial, a Napoleonic fort. The well-documented exhibition is a moving testimony to the suffering and destruction inflicted on the city. There is also a memorial to those who died defending Mount Srđ during the 1991–92 siege of Dubrovnik.

Food and Drink

❶ **LAURA**

Frana Supila 1; tel: 098-428 278; open Sun–Thu 6.30–midnight, Fri–Sat 6.30–2am; €

A small ivy-covered terrace makes this corner bar hard to spot, but it's a favourite place for people who like good music and inexpensive drinks. It gets very lively in the evenings.

Copacabana beach, Babin Kuk

LAPAD, BABIN KUK AND GRUŽ

A walk around the peninsula takes you to the heart of Dubrovnik's summertime playground and some of its most popular beaches. Out of season, the sea views are just as spectacular.

DISTANCE: 4.5km (2.8 miles)
TIME: Half day, but longer if you want to spend the day at the beach
START: Pile Gate
END: Pile Gate
POINTS TO NOTE: Although many visitors will be based at the hotels on the peninsulas, for simplicity's sake this route starts with a 10-minute journey on the No.6 bus from the Pile Gate.

The great majority of Dubrovnik's hotels are to be found on the Lapad and Babin Kuk peninsulas, just a short bus ride from the Old City, and close to Gruž harbour. Although many new developments are changing the face of these suburbs, they remain pleasant, family-friendly, tree-filled areas with delightful bays. This route is a great introduction to the area and encompasses a delightful walk past Lapad Bay and around the Babin Kuk headland.

LAPAD'S PEDESTRIANISED PROMENADE

The bus route runs west from the Pile Gate past the urban bus station and along the southwest side of Gruž harbour, passing the Hotel Lapad (www.hotel-lapad.hr) and some magnificent mansions sitting in palm-shaded gardens, to the Orsan Yacht Club. Here it turns away from the harbour and goes uphill, along **Štalište Kralja Zvonimira**. Get off at the **post office ❶** (ask for the *pošta*) at the roundabout, cross the main road and walk down the attractive, pedestrianised section of Zvonimira towards the sea. You will pass a number of small hotels and a whole line of cafés with comfortable swing seats set out on the tiled pavement. Near the end of the street, a little promenade leads off to the left, parallel to the beach. (It later becomes Masarykov put, a road lined with big hotels that wends its way up to the headland.) On the corner is a park with a children's playground and a row of little kiosks selling tickets for boat trips to the islands.

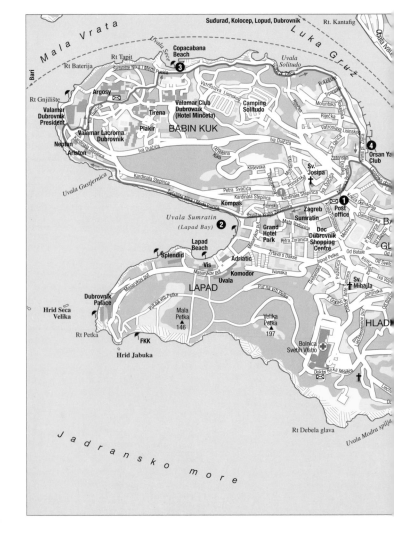

Suđurađ, Kolocep, Lopud, Dubrovnik • Rt. Kantafig

Mala Vrata

Luka Gruž

Bari

Rt Baterija

Rt Tapit

Rt Gnjilište

Šetalište Nika I Meda Pucića

Uvala Seče

Copacabana Beach ③

Uvala Solitudo

Rt. Kantafig

Oxela Naul...

Argosy ✉

Valamar Dubrovnik President

Tirena

Valamar Lacroma Dubrovnik

Vatroslava Lisinskog

Valamar Club Dubrovnik (Hotel Minčeta)

Plakir

Iva Dulčića

Camping Solitudo

BABIN KUK

Moluntska

Riječka

Vatroslav Lisinsko

Zatonska

Neptun

Kardinala Stepinca

Ariston

Iva Dulčića

Od Babina

Iva Dulčića

Klševska

Sv. Josipa ✝

④ Orsan Ya Club

Uvala Gustjernica

Kardinala Stepinca

Petra Svačića

Šetalište Nika I Meda Pucića

Stonska

Kardinala Stepinca

Uvala Sumratin (Lapad Bay) ②

Kompas

Zagreb Sumratin

① Post Office ①

Dalmatinska

B

Lapad Beach

Splendid

Vis

Adriatic

Komodor

Uvala

Grand Hotel Park

Mata Vodopića

Petra Zoranića

Žrtava s Dakse

Dioc Dubrovnik Shopping Centre

Od Batale

Od Svetc

GL

LAPAD

Masarykov put

Ivanska

Dubrovnik Palace

Hrid Seca Velika

Masarykov put

Rt Petka

FKK

Hrid Jabuka

Put Iza vile Petke

Mala Petka 146

Put Iza vile Petke

Velika Petka 197

Sv. Mihajla ✝

Janjinska

HLAD

Bolnica Svetih Vlaho ✚

Rt Debela glava

Doktor Roka Mišetića

Uvala Modra spilja

Jadransko more

Most people staying in Dubrovnik will be in one of the large hotels around Lapad

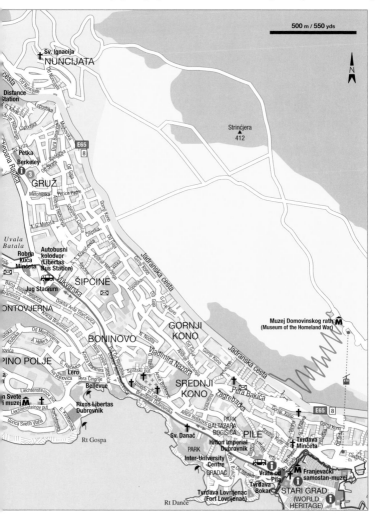

Along Babin Kuk's coastal path

BABIN KUK PENINSULA

Where Zvonimira meets **Uvala Lapad** ❷ (Lapad Bay, shown as Uvala Sumratin on some maps) you will see the big, brash Hotel Kompas (www.adriaticluxuryhotels. com), the Casa Café (http://villa-wolff. hr/restaurant-casa) and the broad beach with its giant concrete slide at the water's edge. You'll also see the beginning of a narrow path on the right that leads westwards along the coast. This is the start of a pleasant walk around the Babin Kuk peninsula, with pine trees framing crystal-clear waters, oleanders drooping from gardens, people fishing from the rocks, cats dozing in the sun and plenty of opportunities to swim from the rocks. Although ladders have been conveniently placed to help you in and out, many of the rocky paths leading to the sea need a certain amount of surefootedness, particularly on the way down.

On your right you'll see the entrance to Restaurant More (www.restaurant-more. com), which belongs to Hotel More (pronounced Mor-eh; www.hotel-more.hr). If you're doing the walk in the late afternoon, this is the place to stop for a drink at the **Cave Bar** (see ❶), which has one of the most stunning interiors you'll see among the local hotels. There's a terrace, too, for al fresco drinks.

At the Levanat restaurant (www.restaurant-levanat.com), the path turns a corner and runs beside the lovely Villa Elita (www.villaelita.com). It carries along the coast to the Hotel Neptun (www. hotelneptundubrovnik.com), where the terrace makes an ideal spot for a drink, especially at sunset. Go round behind the hotel, turn right and then left at the orange Libertas bus sign. You have to make this small detour to avoid the Dubrovnik President/Valamar hotel complex (www.valamar.com), which has colonised the tip of the peninsula.

BABIN KUK'S BEACHES

Now go through a small, family-oriented park, with children's play equipment, table tennis, and benches and stone tables. At the other side, bypass a small shopping centre and follow the path marked 'Plaža/ Beach' a short way down to a little beach known as **Copacabana** ❸. Here you'll find is a sports club, a water chute, pedalos and jet skis for hire, ice-cream sellers and a picturesque café run from a disused chapel. There are very good facilities including showers and changing cabins.

You could stop for a swim or a drink here before carrying on the path before reaching a fork. Veer off to the left and join the narrow pretty path through holm oaks and olive trees, with a view of Daksa island off to the left and the Tudjman Bridge ahead, spanning the estuary. Past a scruffy fishing harbour and the edge of Villa Solitudo campsite (from where you can make diving trips; www.camping-adriatic.com) you come to a line of fishing jetties before the path follows the curve of the coast to the right. It soon joins a residential street and, after a few minutes, you'll see the **Orsan**

Looking across towards Gruž and its giant cruise ships

Yacht Club ❹ on the left. From here you can either take a sharp right up Zvonimira and back to Lapad Bay, or continue along the side of the harbour, back towards the bus station.

Another alternative is to check out the row of bars and cafés on Ulica Ivo Vojnovića that have become the places to flock to in Lapad away from the tourist hot spots. **Mirakul** (see ❷) is one of the most popular. They're all on the Nos. 2, 5, 7 and 9 bus routes.

GRUŽ

Gruž, across the water, does not have a lot to offer the visitor except for lively fruit, vegetable and fish markets (Mon–Sat am), but it is the place to catch the scheduled catamaran to Mljet and the Jadrolinija ferries to Mljet and Korčula and onwards to Split. It's also where the giant cruise ships dock, and this is one of the sites that has been suggested for a new giant aquarium that is supposedly in the pipeline.

The long-distance bus station (Autobusni Kolodvor) is a short way from the harbour. If you have time, though, it is worth a wander, especially in the morning when the area bustles with local life and gives a very different impression of Dubrovnik from the one you will get in the Old Town.

Like Lapad, Gruž is opening more restaurants and cafés that cater for residents as much as for tourists. **Amfora** (see ❸) is worth seeking out.

Food and Drink

❶ CAVE BAR

Kardinala Stepinca 33; 020-494 200; http://hotel-more.hr/4cave_bar_more. php; open daily 10am–11pm; €

The cave in question at the Hotel More's bar was discovered when the hotel was being built, and it lends a highly atmospheric touch to this popular meeting point for guests and non-guests alike. The view from the outdoor terrace overlooking the sea is just as captivating as the grotto-like interior, making it a prime spot for a sundowner.

❷ MIRAKUL

Iva Vojnovića 39; 0 91 534 1962; daily 7am–midnight; €

Dubrovnik's younger set has colonised this lively music bar, which is not to be confused with the pizzeria of the same name in the Old Town. If you're staying in Lapad and want a change from the hotel bars, it's worth a visit to Mirakul or its equally trendy neighbour Culto.

❸ AMFORA

Obala Stjepana Radića 26; tel: 020-419 419; http://amforadubrovnik.com; open daily 8am–midnight; €–€€

It's only a short stroll from Gruž harbour to Amfora, where they show an assured touch with grilled meats, seafood dishes and pastas. Try to get a table on the upstairs terrace, if it's open.

LOKRUM ISLAND

This tiny island of forested footpaths and beaches is only a 15-minute boat journey from Dubrovnik's harbour, but it feels a world away from the bustle of the Old Town.

DISTANCE: 3km (1.8 miles)
TIME: Half day
START: Dubrovnik Old Port
END: Dubrovnik Old Port
POINTS TO NOTE: Boats make the 15-minute journey every hour from the Old Port in summer, from 9am. Some boats to Cavtat also stop off at Lokrum. It can make a leisurely half-day or even a day trip, if you take a picnic or opt to eat in the restaurant. Take swimming things, sunblock and sensible shoes, and don't forget to check the time of the last boat back. If you want to picnic, pick up some freshly baked savoury pastries at the Babić bakery on Frana Supila just outside the Ploče Gate.

Lokrum is a peaceful, undeveloped little island. It is scarcely 2km (1 mile) long, and most things of interest to visitors are within 500 metres/yards of the harbour. However, its chief attraction is its tranquillity and calming greenery. When you arrive at the jetty, there's a map of the island (but none on sale) and a desk where a small entry charge is made, although this is waived for passengers from the regular ferry service.

LEGENDS OF LOKRUM

Legend has it that Richard the Lionheart was shipwrecked here on his way back from the crusades at the end of the 12th century and, in gratitude for his survival, built a votive chapel on the island and financed the construction of Dubrovnik's Cathe-

Game of Thrones fame

Fans of the television series *Game of Thrones* will be very familiar with Lokrum, as the island is the setting for the fictional city of Qarth. There is now a tiny museum displaying some of the paraphernalia from the series, including costumes, inside the Benedictine monastery.

The wooded island is the easiest excursion from Dubrovnik

dral. There is no real evidence for this story, but there may be a grain of truth in it somewhere.

Another legend tells of a curse placed on Lokrum by Benedictine monks in 1808, after the French governor, put in charge by Napoleon when he dissolved the Ragusan Republic, closed the monastery that had been established there in the 11th century. French rule over Dubrovnik did not last long, and when authority passed to the Austro-Hungarian Empire, it seems the curse went with it. Maximilian, brother of Emperor Franz Josef, bought the island in 1859, converted the monastery and established a botanical garden, which is still there today. Some five years later, however, Maximilian was sent off to Mexico as emperor, a position he held only until 1867, when he was assassinated.

Next in line for the curse was Crown Prince Rudolf, son of Franz Josef, who took over the island a dozen years later, but committed suicide in 1889. The lure of Lokrum remained strong, however, and in 1914 Archduke Franz Ferdinand and his wife Sophie planned to spend the summer there. Unfortunately, they went first to Sarajevo, where they were assassinated, and the world was plunged into war.

MONASTERY

Today, Lokrum seems more blessed than cursed. From the jetty at **Portoč ❶**, walk the short distance to the remains of the **monastery ❷**, where there's a restaurant in the cloister, and fig trees cling to the crumbling walls. Be careful if you have children with you: a huge cistern just outside the cloister

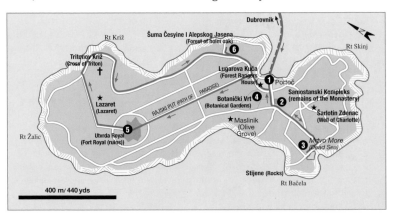

Peacocks roam freely in the Botanical Gardens

is inadequately fenced off. A few hundred metres southeast of the monastery is the **Mrtvo More 3** (Dead Sea), a shallow saltwater lagoon surrounded by flowery shrubs and filled with clear warm water – ideal for swimming. You can also swim off the rocks here and at several other points around the island. Those who prefer calm waters will opt for the lagoon or the little beach near the harbour, while those in search of solitude or more challenging waves will head for the rocks on the southern side. If you find the rocky terrain tough to cope with, you can buy a sponge mat from the kiosk to make lying in the sun more enjoyable. There is also a naturist beach at the southern tip of the island, so look out for the 'FKK' sign if you wish to find it or avoid it.

BOTANICAL GARDENS

Back towards the monastery is the signposted path to the **Botanical Gardens 4**, somewhat overgrown but lush and lovely, as is most of the island. Descendants of the peacocks introduced by Maximilian strut the paths and squawk from their perches in the trees, totally unconcerned by the presence of humans.

FORT ROYAL

If you have the energy you can also climb up to the ruined **Fort Royal 5**, which was built by the French on a hill to the west of the monastery (also signposted). There's not a great deal left of the structure, but the views are splendid and you will be accompanied on your way by butterflies flitting around you and bird calls from above. Be aware of the gaps in the ruins: they're not fenced in and there's no warning of any gaping holes.

FOREST OF HOLM OAK

While you could whizz round the island in a couple of hours, it's worth taking your time strolling through the forested paths taking in the scent of Aleppo pines. Just to the east of Fort Royal is a path through a **forest of holm oak 6**, which leads back to the jetty. Olive trees are scattered around the island, offering blissful shade on a hot day. Part of Lokrum's charm is the fact that no one is allowed to sleep on the island: there's no hotel or campsite, just peace and quiet.

Food and Drink

There are two restaurants next to the monastery. Rajski Vrt, in a lovely shady spot, serves a touristy fare of burgers, pasta and pizzas. Lacroma is a more elegant affair, serving fine Mediterranean cuisine (daily summer 9am–8pm). There is also a small snack bar on the island. Many visitors bring a picnic though, and sit in the shade or on the rocky beach.

Approaching Koločep

THE ELAPHITE ISLANDS

Spend a day island-hopping from Koločep to Šipan and Lopud – three peaceful and pretty Elaphite Islands that lie just north of Dubrovnik. A ferry connects them all, as do private boat excursions.

DISTANCE: 17km (10.5 miles)
TIME: Full day
START: Gruž harbour
END: Gruž harbour
POINTS TO NOTE: Scheduled ferries run from Gruž harbour to the Elaphite islands several times a day in summer, but in order to see all three islands it is easier to take one of the excursions that are advertised all over the city. You can opt for one that offers lunch in a Lopud restaurant or a so-called 'fish picnic' on board, or you can be independent and spend your time on the islands as you wish. If you are in Dubrovnik for an extended stay, you could always decide to return later by ferry to the island you liked best.

This archipelago – of which only three islands are inhabited – gives you a relaxing view of rural life. There is not a great deal to do on any of them apart from walking, eating, drinking, swimming and taking in the scenery, but the islands are a tranquil antidote to Dubrovnik in high season.

THE JOURNEY

Most boat trips start from the harbour at Gruž, from where it is 35–40 minutes to Koločep, the first and smallest of the islands. Look back to land and you will see, above the mouth of the estuary, the striking **Franjo Tuđman Bridge** (named after independent Croatia's first president Franjo Tuđman, who died in 1999), carrying traffic towards Split and Zagreb. As you travel up the coast you will notice how bleak the hillsides are, yellow with broom in early summer but otherwise quite bare and stark. This makes the luxuriant wooded islands, when you reach them, all the more attractive.

A short way out to sea you pass **Daksa**, which belongs to the Elaphite chain but is uninhabited. In the 14th century, it had been the site of a Franciscan monastery, but it has since achieved a more modern notoriety. In October 1944, the Yugoslav Partisans executed 48 people, including the mayor of Dubrovnik, whom they suspected of sympathising with the Nazis. Their remains were discovered as recently as 2009. The current owner of

the island has been trying to sell it, so far with no luck.

KOLOČEP

This is the smallest of the inhabited Elaphite Islands, much of it covered in pine forests and with only about 150 people living in the two main settlements. On reaching **Koločep ❶**, boats dock at **Donje Čelo**, a pretty little harbour with terracotta-roofed houses and a narrow strip of sandy beach that is shared by the Kalamota Island Resort (formerly known as Hotel Villas Koločep). There's also the 13th-century Ascension of Mary Church, a few cafés and, at the far end, the Villa Ruža Restaurant (www.villa-ruza.com) in an old stone building, with tables set out beneath pine trees.

If you come here under your own steam, you could take the path through fragrant lemon and orange orchards, pine forests and olive groves to the other little settlement, **Gornje Čelo ❷**. But if you're on an excursion, you won't have time to do much more than walk the length of the harbour, pop into the souvenir shop, and have a quick dip in the sea and a coffee in one of the cafés by the jetty.

If you're staying on Koločep in self-catering accommodation, bear in mind that there are very few places on the island to buy fresh food. Most provisions are delivered from the mainland every morning – including fresh bread, which normally doesn't arrive until mid-morning. It's worth stocking up on as much fresh food as you can carry before boarding the ferry on the mainland.

ŠIPAN

Many boats go next to Šipan, the furthest island (about 45 minutes), leav-

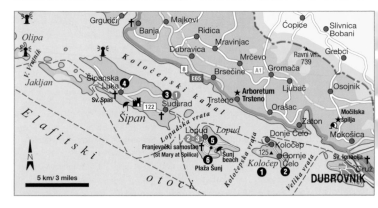

Lunch in sleepy Suđurađ

ing Lopud as the last stop so that passengers have the most time there for lunch, swimming and exploration. Some trips ignore Šipan altogether, but this is a pity; it is worth taking a tour that includes it, even if for only a brief stop.

Šipan is the largest of the islands but is the least developed for tourism. It had been one of the preferred spots for 15th-century Dubrovnik aristocracy to build summer residences; at the height of the island's popularity, there were more than 40 that were built. Nowadays, it is more agricultural than the other islands in the chain, and its once-flourishing olive groves and oil production are being revived. However, the population is low – fewer than 500 – and it is hard to imagine young people staying here once they grow up. Scheduled ferries and excursion boats stop at **Suđurađ** ❸, to the southeast, a tiny harbour where houses shelter beneath vines, olives are cultivated on small terraces and gardens are bright with flowers. A little snack bar at the end of the harbour holds a huge olive press and grinding wheel and has an inviting open hearth that keeps the family warm in winter. If you want a superior lunch, book one of the tables by the harbour at the restaurant at **Hotel Božica** (see ❶).

Two sturdy towers looming up above the harbour belong to the 16th-century summer residence of wealthy ship-owner Vice Stjepović-Skočibuha. Approach it from the steps on the other side and you will be able to see down into its cultivated gardens.

If you have time (but you won't if you are on a 'three islands trip'), you could walk to **Šipanska Luka** ❹, the island's other port, about 5km (3 miles) to the northwest. More shadows of Šipan's former glory are dotted about here, including remains of an old duke's palace and what is thought to be a Roman villa. The walk to Šipanska Luka is a pleasant one as you dawdle past olive groves and small vineyards edged with dry-stone walls. The island can get extremely busy in the height of summer with day-trippers, but in temperate months such as September, it's blissfully peaceful.

LOPUD

Lopud is the final stop, about 15 minutes later. During the Ragusan Republic this was a thriving port, with a population more than 10 times that of today – which is around 220. It produced several Admirals of the Fleet

---

Deer islands

Elaphite means deer, but the deer population on the islands is long gone. There are rumours of wild boar on Šipan, however. Similarly, the human population has dwindled from several thousand to about 850. Lopud alone used to have 4,000; now there are just over 400.

and was the birthplace of ship-owner and merchant Miho Pracat (1528–1607) who, after coming close to financial ruin following two disastrous voyages, finally made a fortune. This he left to the Republic when he died without an heir. There is just one settlement on Lopud now – the little port of the same name built around a sandy bay – but it is increasingly attracting visitors who make it their holiday base, staying in one of the hotels or in the private rooms and apartments you will see on offer. If you enjoy tranquillity, it is a perfect place to stay, especially as no cars are allowed on the island. It is only 55 minutes from Dubrovnik via the direct ferry, and the last ferry in summer runs from the city late in the evening. However, if you were unlucky enough to experience a spell of bad weather, you could feel pretty isolated here as the pace of life on the island is very slow. Out of season, there is even less to do and see.

IN THE PORT

Disembarking from the ferry, get your bearings by turning left above the **port** ❺, past the post office and the elegant Hotel Villa Vilina (www.villa-vilina.hr) to visit the church of **St Mary of Spilica** (Gospa od Spilica). It is attached to a Franciscan monastery established here in 1483, which served as a place of refuge for the islanders as well as performing a religious function. The church has some beautiful paintings and 15th-century carved choir stalls, as well as lovely cloisters.

A HARBOUR WALK

Back at the harbour, refresh yourself with an ice cream and a cold drink at **Palma** (see ❷). At the jetty there is a small museum and treasury on the other side of the road, but they are usually closed. Walk the length of the oleander-lined harbour towards the modern Hotel Lafodia (www.lafodia-hotel.com) at the far end, which has a pool, its own jetty and perfect views of the other islands. En route you will see, beside an imposing but usually closed church, a sign saying Grand Hotel. Venture up the palm-shaded drive through the overgrown gardens and you will find a concrete, modernist building, constructed in 1936 as a sign on the wall informs you, but now deserted and looking decidedly forlorn. There are plans to renovate and reopen the hotel, but funds do not seem to be forthcoming at present. Close by are two tiny chapels, one dedicated to St Jerome, who was born in Dalmatia; the other, the Chapel of the Holy Cross, belonged to Miho Pracat, and his home is believed to have been next door. All that stands there now is a derelict cottage.

You could choose to have lunch in one of the attractive restaurants that line the harbour. **Konoba Dubrovnik**

Along the Lopud waterfront

is a friendly place right by the water's edge (see ❸). Wherever you decide to eat, if you're there in high season you might want to book a table for lunch soon after you arrive rather than waiting for lunchtime when tables fill up rapidly. Little paths lead off the harbour and climb up the hillside, from where you get wonderful views of the coastline and the nearby islands if you take a post-prandial stroll.

ACROSS THE ISLAND

Afterwards, take the path marked **Plaža Šunj** ❻ beside the Grand Hotel and follow it for about half an hour through pine-scented woods, with conveniently situated benches, to the lovely, sandy Šunj Bay. The water is shallow and safe for children – it's only about knee deep for a good 100 or so metres/yards. There are a couple of summer cafés serving simple food, toilets and showers, and loungers and parasols for hire. There is also an electric golf cart taxi that can transport people with limited mobility for a fee. It's usually waiting at the harbour, so look out for it when you dock.

But don't imagine that it's going to be a secluded spot just because it was a bit of a hike to get here. All excursion boat passengers will have been advised that it's the best beach on the island, and one of the few sandy ones to be found in Croatia's Adriatic coast and islands – something that local people know well.

Those who are staying on Lopud have the pleasure of knowing that when the last boat departs for Dubrovnik, the beach will be all theirs.

Food and Drink

❶ HOTEL BOŽICA

Suđurađ 3, Šipan; tel: 020-0325 400; www.hotel-bozica.hr; €–€€

Locally grown organic produce including olives and fresh fish figure prominently on the menu of this classy hotel restaurant. It's in a prime position on a terrace close to Suđurađ's pretty little harbour – all the better to enjoy delicious Ston oysters and wines from the Pelješac peninsula.

❷ PALMA

Obala Ive Kuljevana, Lopud; tel: 091-928 0951; €

This busy café overlooking the harbour makes some of the best ice cream you'll find in the region. If you're feeling particularly hungry, try one of their giant stacked ice-cream desserts.

❸ KONOBA DUBROVNIK

Obala Ive Kuljevana 40, Lopud; tel: 020-759 172; €–€€

Right by the water's edge at the harbour is this relaxed, family-run restaurant serving good-quality seafood and Dalmatian meat dishes. It's worth booking in advance during the summer, even by only a few hours.

A third of Mljet is protected as a national park

MLJET

Mljet is a beautiful island to the northwest of Dubrovnik. It makes a delightful day out from the city, but there is accommodation if you want to stay longer.

DISTANCE: 10km (6.2 miles)
TIME: Full day
START: Polače harbour, Mljet
END: Polače harbour
POINTS TO NOTE: The catamaran *Nona Ana* leaves Gruž harbour and takes about 90 minutes to reach Polače. Tickets can't be bought in advance, so during high season it's best to be at the ferry port an hour before sailing. Tickets are available at the small white kiosk across the road from the Jadrolinija ferry office. If you're spending just one day on Mljet, make sure you get off at the second port, Polače, not at Sobra on the eastern end of the island. Take swimming gear and a picnic if you don't want to eat at one of the restaurants. Several agencies run excursions to Mljet, but getting there under your own steam is not difficult.

Unlike the bare mainland coastline, Mljet (pronounced *Mlyet*) is richly forested and offers much welcome shade on a hot day. Unspoilt, wild and beautiful, it covers roughly 100 sq km (38 sq miles); the western end, where the catamaran will dock, is a National Park that was established in 1960. Its area of 31 sq km (12 sq miles) encompasses several small settlements, the port of Pomena, and the hotels and restaurants within them, as well as the lakes and surrounding terrain.

POLAČE

Polače's ❶ ruined Roman walls give little clue that a palace second in size only to Diocletian's in Split had stood here – hence the name Polače. Even during the height of the season, the place remains a sleepy Adriatic fishing village. Its large bay is sheltered by four islets, Tajnik, Moračnik, Ovrata and Kobrava. There are a few small restaurants here of varying quality, but you might want to save yourself for lunch in Pomena if you don't bring your own food for a picnic in the National Park.

NATIONAL PARK

To get to **Mljet National Park ❷** (http://np-mljet.hr), you can hire a bike directly

Polače harbour restaurant

opposite the jetty at Polače, or a beach buggy or scooter from Mini Brum 100 metres/yards or so to the left (www.rent-a-car-scooter-mljet.hr), but most people head for the park kiosk just to the right. Here you pay your entrance fee (currently 125 kuna Jun–Sep, 70 kuna rest of the year), which includes minibus transport to and from the park, and the boat fare out to Sveta Marija (St Mary's Island). The fee may seem a bit steep, and it has increased quite sharply, but all the profits are ploughed back into the upkeep of the park. (Incidentally, if you make your own way to the park entrance you still pay the same amount.)

ST MARY'S ISLAND

A five-minute bus ride takes you to **Pristanište ❸** on the shore of **Veliko Jezero** (Big Lake), actually a tidal expanse of saltwater, fed by the sea. Here you can board a small boat that will take you out to the island of **Sveta Marija ❹** (St Mary). The Benedictine monastery and church here

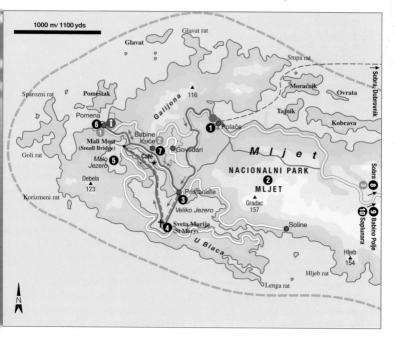

Pine groves provide much-needed shade

have a chequered architectural history. The church and parts of the monastery are Romanesque and date from the 12th century, but there were 14th-century additions and a lot of changes in the subsequent two centuries, when it was given a Renaissance façade. After the monks abandoned the place in 1808, it fell into disrepair and is now being renovated by the St Mary's Foundation, in conjunction with the Diocese of Dubrovnik, to which it was handed back in 1997 under the Law of Returned Property. The church, an imposing single-naved structure, is coming along nicely and can be visited, but the monastery and cloister are still under wraps and closed to visitors. However, the ground floor functions as the Restaurant Melita, right on the water's edge. The food can be disappointing but the setting is beautiful.

Take a wander along the shady island paths, which won't take more than about 15 minutes, even if you stop to visit the two little votive chapels, built by grateful sailors who had survived watery misfortunes. If you've brought your swimming gear, take a dip off the rocks and dry out in the sun before getting the boat back to shore. The trip will not go directly to your starting point, but will take you to Mali Most (Small Bridge) on the edge of **Malo Jezero** ❺ (Small Lake). Here there's a small swimming beach and opportunities to rent kayaks, canoes and rowing boats, popular activities for those who want to be on the water rather than in it.

POMENA

A path marked 'Pomena' – all the park's paths are clearly signposted – takes you round the side of Malo Jezero along on a pleasant route, easy underfoot, bordered by pines and olive trees, and with bright yellow butterflies fluttering along ahead of you. After a while the path leaves the lake and goes up a fairly gentle wooded hill, then descends to the little settlement of **Pomena** ❻. Once a tiny fishing village, it is now Mljet's tourist centre – but a restrained and pretty one. The Hotel Odisej dominates the bay. The name (Odyssey) relates to the popular myth that Ulysses stopped on Mljet during his voyage – one of several southern European countries to lay the same claim. Some smart yachts bob in the little bay, and there are several modest restaurants, as well as the one attached to the hotel.

Follow a path round to the right of the harbour to find a row of little eating places. Lobster is advertised at many restaurants on the island but, as everywhere else, it is expensive and is usually priced by the kilo. There's plenty of other seafood, though, and at good prices, and Pomena would make a delightful lunch stop if you didn't eat on the island. **Barba Ive** (see ❶) is a good bet. There are more opportunities to rent buggies here from Mini Brum, many of them painted to resemble tigers, zebras or monkeys, and bikes can be hired from the hotel.

St Mary's Island   *Ulysses Cave*

BACK TO THE BOAT

When you are ready to head back the 2.5 km (1.5 miles) to Pristanište to pick up the minibus, retrace your steps as far as Mali Most and continue along the lake shore. You will pass a pretty settlement, **Babine Kuće ❼**, where there is another opportunity to eat or drink at **Konoba Mali Raj** (see ❷), on a geranium-clad terrace beneath a vine. Don't linger too long, as there's only one boat back. If you have time and can't resist the lure of the lakes, you can pass the pick-up point and clamber down to the water's edge for another swim. As long as there are no signs prohibiting swimming, and you are not near the seaward exit from the lake where the current is strong, you may swim anywhere.

Back in Polače, you could wander around the ruined walls of the Roman palace to the right of the National Park kiosk, but this won't detain you for long. Better to sit in one of the cafés that line the waterfront, enjoy the smell of wood smoke as restaurateurs fire up their barbecues, and sample the local dessert wine, prošek, while you wait for boarding time.

This route has been designed for those who only have a day to spare. If you have longer, there is a wealth of trails to explore in the park, none of them too taxing, although there are a few steep gradients. You can buy a map with marked trails from one of the official kiosks. There are also several sandy beaches to visit on the eastern side of the island. If you plan to stay for more than a day, check www.croatia-mljet-apartment.com for accommodation. If you miss the boat back to Dubrovnik, you will have to knock on one of the doors advertising a *sobe* – a room for rent.

EASTERN MLJET

Visitors planning to spend more time on Mljet can take the ferry from Dubrovnik to **Sobra ❽**, the main port on the eastern side of the island. Ferries run all year round to this little fishing village of stone houses in a sheltered bay backed by steep hills. There's no beach, but that doesn't stop people from swimming off the rocks. There are a few restaurants and a market, as well as a handful of guesthouses, rooms to rent and self-catering apartments, some of which are set on the hillside with lovely sea views. It's sleepy, relaxed and pleasantly slow – just as you would expect in such a small settlement.

About 6km (3.7 miles) from Sobra is **Babino Polje ❾**, one of the island's oldest villages. It sits in the shadow of the island's highest peak, Veliki Grad (514 metres/yards), while below are the fertile fields that give the village its name. Veliki Grad is also on a well-marked hiking trail that starts in Pomena, curves up to Polače and eventually snakes across the island for 40km (25 miles) to Sobra. The views from Veliki Grad stretch as far as the mainland and neighbouring islands, and are worth the hike up the scrubby hillside. Babino Polje is actually three hamlets – Zadublje, Srčenovići and Zabriježe – of old stone houses clustered together.

Sunbathing near the canal entrance to Veliko Jezero, Big Lake

There are several campsites in the area, as is **Sutmiholjska**, a soft pebbly beach tucked into a narrow cove a few kilometres away on the southern coast. The pine groves backing the beach offer some wonderful shade on a hot day. Facilities are minimal, so you might want to bring your own supplies.

Food and Drink

① BARBA IVE

Pomena 4; tel: 098-669 662;
www.konobabarbaive.com; €–€€
For fish so fresh it still twitches, head to this friendly waterfront restaurant for beautifully cooked dishes including octopus stew and seafood risotto. Meat-eaters are catered for too, with plenty of Dalmatian specialities including *pršut*.

② KONOBA MALI RAJ

Babine Kuće 3; tel: 091-584 4940;
http://maliraj-mljet.com/en; €
This is a lovely spot for a drink before heading back to Polače to catch the catamaran. Or if you have time for lunch, try the grilled squid.

③ VILLA MIROSA

Saplunara; tel: 099-199 6270;
www.villa-mirosa.com; €
A short walk from Saplunara beach this welcoming restaurant and guesthouse serves home-cooked food (and self-caught fish) on the covered terrace. Unusually for Croatia, vegetarians are also catered for.

Not far from Sutmiholjska beach is Ulysses Cave – one of many caves along this limestone karst coast, although this one is said to have sheltered Ulysses on his lengthy odyssey. Fearless locals make use of the raised shoreline around the cave and jump straight into the sparkling blue water and swim into the grotto. There are lower points from which to jump if you're not quite so fearless.

For a country where sandy beaches are rare, it's unusual to find three very close to each other – and on a relatively small island. At Mljet's southernmost point is an oddly shaped peninsula, into which one of its many indents is **Limuni** beach (also called Uvala Blaće). Fingers of pine forests arc protectively around the beach of fine sand, which has a long shallow section of clear blue-green water. It can be reached by road, even if the last part of it isn't paved.

Slightly more accessible is its near neighbour, **Saplunara** ⑩. You won't find many facilities here, but you will find Aleppo pines and two beaches of soft sand. There's also a shingle beach closer to the centre. The village itself is very small (population around 32), but it does offer a few guesthouses and private rooms. The restaurant at the **Villa Mirosa** is worth a visit (see ③).

If you plan to spend a few days on the island, you'll have to consider transport. The public bus service is patchy at best. There are buses that connect the two ferry ports, but they're on a limited schedule and not that reliable. Car hire is easy to arrange in the main villages, and hiring a scooter is easier, cheaper and often more practical.

Along Cavtat's stunning waterfront

CAVTAT

*Take the boat from Dubrovnik's Old Port to this pretty
village where restaurants line the quayside and a
pleasant wooded path circles the peninsula.*

DISTANCE: 3km (1.8 miles)
TIME: Half day
START: Cavtat Harbour
END: Cavtat Harbour
POINTS TO NOTE: In summer, boats leave Dubrovnik's Old Port for Cavtat throughout the day. The regular service takes about 45 minutes, but some boats stop at points along the coast and take longer – check when you book. The last boat back from Cavtat is usually about 5.30pm. There is also a bus service (no.10), which is a good choice – and much cheaper – if the sea is rough.

Cavtat is an attractive village about 17km (10 miles) south of Dubrovnik, on a peninsula between two bays. It was the site of first a Greek, then a Roman settlement of Epidaurus and the place from which the Illyrian inhabitants fled in the 7th century to found Ragusa. The foundations of a fort on the tip of the peninsula are all that remain of the Roman period.

A visit to Cavtat (pronounced *Tsavtat*) is one of the most popular day trips from Dubrovnik. Its proximity to the airport makes it a good option if you have an early flight, but the village is also an appealing destination in its own right, with a relaxed atmosphere and good restaurants and cafés. Many visitors prefer to base themselves in Cavtat and either take the boat or the more economical bus into Dubrovnik. Although the boats stop running relatively early, the buses carry on all evening, giving you the chance to experience a different side of Dubrovnik in the evening once the crowds have gone back to their cruise ships.

During July and August, Cavtat holds many events during its summer festival, including concerts with male voice choirs and folklore groups, as well as water polo tournaments. In September, it's time for the Epidaurus Festival, a celebration of classical music and the arts in general. And in February, the town puts on its own pre-Lenten carnival.

As your boat approaches the harbour, you will have a picture-postcard view of a palm-lined promenade with a church at either end, and inviting-looking restaurants and cafés in between. Depend-

ing on the time of day, you might even catch some water polo teams practising in one cordoned-off area of the port.

To the right, as you disembark, is the parish church of **St Nicholas** 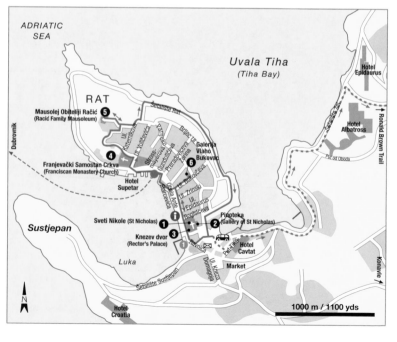 (Sveti Nikole) and, signposted on the road to the left, the **Gallery of St Nicholas** ❷ (Pinoteka; open daily 10am–1pm). Beside the church, the **Rector's Palace** ❸ contains a gallery (Mon–Fri 9am–1pm) housing the library and paintings, costumes and other items collected by Vlaho Bogišić, a writer and lawyer born here in

1834, whose bulky statue sits opposite. Beside him is a triangle of restaurants, of which the best known is **Leut** (see ❶).

MONASTERY AND MAUSOLEUM

Going back along the harbourfront, picking your way between restaurant tables, and passing the attractive little Hotel Supetar, you reach the **Franciscan Monastery Church** ❹ (Franjevački Samostan Crkva; usually open; free). The eye-catching polyptych of St Michael (1510) to

Cavtat's rooftops and mountainous interior

the left of the door is the work of Vicko Dobričević, son of Lovro (see route 1). One oddity in this plain and peaceful little church (although it is not uncommon in Croatia) is a disembodied hand appearing from the pulpit, holding a crucifix.

Behind the church, turn left into Ulica Katernikova, then continue up a flight of steps to the hilltop cemetery, dominated by the **Račić Family Mausoleum** ❺ (Apr–Oct Mon–Sat 10am–5pm). This octagonal, white marble structure was designed in 1922 by Ivan Meštrović, the best-known 20th-century Croatian sculptor, for the super-wealthy ship-owning family. Its bronze doors, with images of four Slav saints, are guarded by a pair of Art Nouveau-style angels, while another angel flexes his wings on the cupola. The Račićs, who followed each other to the mausoleum in quick succession in the 1920s, obviously wanted to appear as opulent in death as they were in life.

AROUND THE PENINSULA

After admiring the sweeping views up and down the coast, leave the cemetery by the back gate and follow a sloping path through pine woods. Where the path divides, you could take the right fork and follow it around the outside of town, to arrive back at the church of St Nicholas. Better, though, to take the steps down to a bathing area, where there's a beach café and you can rent sunloungers and umbrellas during the summer. Here a concreted path continues along the waterside to Cavtat's second bay, Uvala Tiha. This is the pick-up and drop-off point for coaches and public buses.

The road parallel to the bay, past the police station and a small branch of the tourist office, soon becomes quieter, more rural, and is lined with cypresses. The road then widens out again when it reaches the Hotel Albatros, looking a bit like a terracotta cruise ship built around a swimming pool. A short distance further along, at the Hotel Epidaurus, the path peters out altogether.

Another option would be to bypass the walk up to the cemetery and take a gentle stroll under umbrella pines around the 7km (4.3km) smooth shaded path that hugs the peninsula.

A DETOUR

Those with more time, strong walking shoes and plenty of energy may like to try the Ronald Brown Pathway, which starts behind the Hotel Albatros and leads to a cross on a hilltop. This marks the spot where the plane carrying the US Secretary of Commerce and the rest of a trade delegation to Croatia crashed in 1996. The trail takes at least two hours, and winds steeply uphill. The narrowness and terrain of the path make it unsuitable when bad weather strikes, as clouds can descend very quickly. Anyone walking the trail would be advised to wear proper footwear.

The waterfront is lined with palm trees, restaurants and cafés

BUKOVAC'S GALLERY

Now return to the harbour for lunch, if you haven't already done so. Lunch over, take the fifth little lane on your right from the promenade, Ulica Bukovčeva, to the **Galerija Vlaho Bukovac** ⬤ (open Nov–Mar Tues–Sat 9am–1pm, 4–5pm, Sun 2–5pm, Apr–Oct Mon–Sat 9am–6pm, Sun 9am–2pm), dedicated to Bukovac (1855–1922), the highly esteemed and prolific artist who was born here. Bukovac had a hard early life, but was accepted by the Paris École des Beaux-Arts after gaining the financial backing of the enlightened Bishop Strossmayer. The artist worked for many years in Zagreb before becoming a professor at the Prague Academy.

The ground floor of the house is empty except for some modern paintings, but the walls and staircases throughout are colour-washed and decorated with friezes depicting birds, animals and rural scenes – all done by Bukovac. Upstairs, two large rooms display many of his portraits, mostly of family members – detailed, contemplative and extremely memorable. One chilling picture, in a room by itself, apparently shows the heads of the artist and his wife lying on a table, looking up at those of four children, suspended by their hair.

Enjoy a coffee on the seafront while you watch your boat appearing over the horizon. A word of warning: if the sea gets really choppy, the smaller boats will not make the journey, so you will have to go back by bus. This is no great hardship: bus No.10 runs regularly from the terminal in Tiha Bay, where a timetable is posted, to Dubrovnik bus station, with stops en route. The journey takes about half an hour.

The region south of Cavtat, down to Montenegro, is Konavle, a rich agricultural district where the silk moth is cultivated. This silk used in local costumes worn on Sundays in the village of Čilipi. Hillside hamlets make up Pridvorje, a town eulogised by Dubrovnik's Renaissance poets. There's a Franciscan monastery and a former palace of the rector of Konavle. If you don't have your own transport, the region can be explored on a Jeep safari, an organised food and folklore tour, a guided jaunt on a quad bike or a ride on a scenic tourist train through the vineyards. Bicycle hire is easy to arrange in Cavtat, which is the starting point for a 9.5km (6 miles) route to Čilipi. It is also home to the **Konavle Heritage Museum** (open Mon–Sat 9am–1pm, 5–8pm, Sun 9am–2pm) with a collection of folk costumes, textiles and embroidery.

Food and Drink

❶ LEUT

Trumbićev put 17; tel: 020-478 477;
www.restaurant-leut.com; €€–€€€
Leut has been run by the same family since 1971. Its waterside location is a beautiful backdrop to seafood dishes that are rich in lobster and prawns. Reservations are advisable for weekends and in high season, especially for Sunday lunch. Open Mar–Nov 11am–midnight.

Arboretum fountain, Trsteno

TRSTENO AND STON

Take a trip up the coast to visit one of Croatia's oldest botanical gardens, and onwards to the twin villages of Ston and Mali Ston to sample some of the best oysters in the country.

DISTANCE: 55km (34 miles) by car each way

TIME: Full day

START: Dubrovnik

END: Dubrovnik

POINTS TO NOTE: It would be best to hire a car for this trip, as buses to Ston are infrequent, and you might like to combine it with a stay in Korčula (see route 11). If you just want to visit Trsteno, the bus to Split which leaves approximately every hour from the long-distance bus station at Gruž harbour will drop you off there, and will also stop at Zaton.

Trsteno is a tiny village about 18km (11 miles) up the coast from Dubrovnik that has gained a wide reputation for its Arboretum. The drive runs along a beautiful stretch of coast with good views across a number of islands including Mljet in the distance and the Elaphite Islands.

The twin villages of Ston and Mali Ston on the Pelješac peninsula are known principally for having some of the best oysters in the world and for their huge defensive walls, claimed to be second only to the Great Wall of China.

SEASIDE STOP IN ZATON

If you are driving, follow signs to Split, which take you up above the town and across the Tudjman Bridge. From there it's a pleasant 10-km (6-mile) drive to **Zaton ❶**, set in a deep bay that causes the highway to scuttle inland around farmland. Zaton is divided in two: Veliki (Large) and Mali (Small), and together they form an attractive little settlement that is building up its tourist infrastructure, catering to those who want to be outside Dubrovnik but within easy reach of the city. There are a number of residences that were once the summer retreats of wealthy families. If you're here around lunchtime, stop at **Restaurant Gverović-Orsan** (see ❶), set in an old boathouse, after which it is named.

TRSTENO ARBORETUM

Some 8km (5 miles) further on you reach **Trsteno**, where two huge 500-year-old plane trees dominate the main street. You can't miss them: their diameters are about five metres (16 feet). Turn left beside the trees down a narrow road and you will shortly reach the **Arboretum ❷** (open May–Oct: daily 7am–7pm; Nov–Apr 8am–4pm), which now belongs to the Croatian Academy of Science and the Arts. Established as a summer home and garden in the late 15th century by Ivan Gučetić, a prominent member

of Ragusa's nobility, it has changed and expanded over the years and now covers an area of 25 hectares (63 acres). The collection includes more than 300 species of trees, shrubs and plants, some rare and exotic, in a delightful setting running down to the sea. This makes a lovely, shady place to spend some time on a hot summer's day. Fans of the *Game of Thrones* television series will certainly recognise the setting as the King's Landing palace gardens.

Towards the end of 1991, the Arboretum came under a dual attack from sea and air, and much of it was

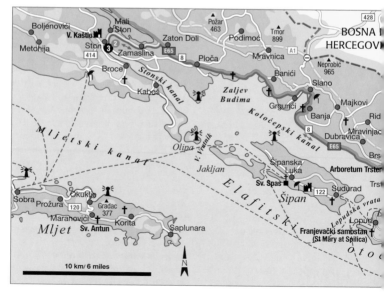

Picturesque Trsteno harbour

destroyed in the subsequent fire, although the oldest part escaped without too much damage. A great deal of restoration has been done since then, and the garden, a mixture of formal and semi-wild areas, is delightful – as is the over-the-top, 18th-century Neptune's Grotto, with dolphin fountains and water lilies. If you are driving, park in the designated area and you will see nearby a sign pointing towards a little beach to which you can make your way if you feel like a swim after you have explored the garden. As parking can be difficult at peak times, you might want to have a drink at the café at the garden's entrance and leave your car in the café's car park.

STON

Follow the coast for another 30km (18 miles) or so and you will come to **Ston** ❸, which, like Zaton, is divided in two. The larger village is sometimes called Veliki (Large) Ston, and the smaller is always known as Mali (Little) Ston. They sit at the head of the Pelješac peninsula, divided by a narrow isthmus. The 5km (3 miles) of great walls that connect the two (and for which World Heritage status is being sought) were built in the 14th century, principally to protect the salt pans, which you will see as you drive between the two settlements. Still in use today (you can buy little cloth bags of Ston salt, which make a nice souvenir), the salt pans were once vital to Ragusa's economy and were much coveted by Napoleon. The energetic can climb the walls from Veliki Ston for fabulous views of the salt pans and the surrounding area.

You reach Mali Ston first, but save this for later and turn left instead, and drive about 2km (1 mile) to Ston. The Veliki is a misnomer: although it's called a town, and it has a long history, having been founded in 1333, it is not much more than a village, with a population of scarcely 600. Ston has little to offer in the way of sites

Mali Ston fisherman

or entertainment, but it's an appealing and friendly little place with several churches and a morning market. The café tables set out in the central square, shaded by lime trees and flowering shrubs, make it a good place to stop for coffee. The area was badly hit by an earthquake in 1996 (fortunately with no loss of life), and there are still some signs of damage, but much of it has been well repaired.

Food and Drink

❶ RESTAURANT GVEROVIĆ-ORSAN
Štikovica 43, Zaton Mali; tel: 098-271 555; www.gverovic-orsan.hr; daily Mar–Dec 12pm–12am; €–€€
Savour squid-ink risotto and prawn gnocchi in a peaceful location right by the water's edge, where you can have a swim afterwards. This is an appealing option for lunch even if you return to Dubrovnik immediately afterwards, so it's best to book ahead during the season.

❷ KAPETANOVA KUĆA
Obala Dr Ante Starčevića, Mali Ston; tel: 020-754 555; www.ostrea.hr; €–€€
This waterside restaurant gets busy in the summer, so book ahead to enjoy Ston oysters and fresh seafood as well as excellent wines from wineries in the Pelješac peninsula.

OYSTER CENTRAL

Return now to Mali Ston, which is tiny, just a cluster of houses around a fortified tower, set beside a bay that gives the place its *raison d'être* – oysters. In 1936, the General Trades International Exhibition awarded these oysters the Grand Prix, declaring them the best in the world. You will have seen the expanses of oyster beds as you approach the village.

The best-known restaurant, the Villa Koruna (see page 103), displays a certificate awarded at the 1936 exhibition. That seems a very long time ago, and many things have changed since then, but the oysters – and the mussels – still rank among the best and bring flocks of people here for Sunday lunch. And lunch is what you will probably be interested in as well.

If the Koruna – with its huge tanks of fish and a couple of slowly circling turtles – is busy with tour groups, as it sometimes is, walk round to the left of it, past the great tower. Here you will find the **Taverna Bota Šare** (see page 103) and **Kapetanova Kuča** (see ❷), both of which offer excellent seafood at tables right beside the bay. If you are not a big fan of oysters, don't worry, there's plenty more on the menu to choose from: garlicky mussels, black risotto (made with squid ink) and lobster soup, to mention just a few.

Walled Korčula Town

KORČULA

This fertile island northwest of Dubrovnik is a destination in its own right, but can be visited in a day in this excursion that concentrates on the walled town of Korčula itself.

DISTANCE: 1.5km (0.9 miles)
TIME: Full day
START: Korčula harbour
END: Korčula harbour
POINTS TO NOTE: You can get to the island by ferry (about 3.5 hours) or by faster catamaran if you go on an organised excursion. But if you come in winter, or would like to spend more than a few hours here, you could hire a car, drive the 115km (70 miles) then make the 15-minute ferry crossing from Orebić, from where boats do operate in winter. You could then spend the night here and perhaps combine the trip with a visit to Ston and Trsteno.

Korčula, which is 48 nautical miles northwest of Dubrovnik, is lush and bountiful. Like the Pelješac peninsula from which it is separated by a narrow channel, it specialises in wine production. This area produces some of the best wine in Croatia, but most of it is for domestic consumption so will be unfamiliar to visitors. The best beaches are on the south of the island, and are worth exploring if you are here on an extended stay.

GETTING TO THE ISLAND

Shortly after the town of Prizdrina the vineyards end, the landscape becomes barer and rockier, and ahead you see the glittering sea, framing the island of Korčula. The port of Orebić, from where you take the ferry, is small, but there are several hotels and to the north are some of the coast's best sandy beaches, which are popular with windsurfers. There are car ferries from here, but if you plan to concentrate on the town of Korčula, as this itinerary does, it would be as well to leave your car here and take the passenger ferry across. The Old Town itself is pedestrianised, and outlying areas are easily reached on foot. As your boat takes you across the narrow channel, the walled town, with its four sturdy towers, honey-coloured walls and terracotta roofs, resembles a fairy-tale city.

Once in the harbour (don't forget to check on return boat times), you will see straight ahead of you a broad flight of

Cannon guarding the waterfront

steps, dividing around a central fountain. This is **Primorska Vrata** ❶ (Sea Gate), one of two entrances to the Old Town, but before going in you may like to pop into the adjacent tourist office, which is set in a splendid 16th-century loggia. If you are going to stay the night on the island, the elegant Hotel Korčula next door is a good choice.

THE OLD TOWN

At the top of the steps a broad terrace is lined with café tables and straight ahead, a narrow alley (Ulica Dinka Miroševiča) leads up to **St Mark's Square** where you will find the Cathedral, the Treasury Museum and the Town Museum. The Gothic-Renaissance **St Mark's Cathedral** ❷ (Katedrala Sveti Marka; opening times vary) is constructed, like most of Korčula's buildings, from the mellow limestone that made the island, and its stone masters, prosperous and famous. The tower and cupola, dating from around 1480, are the work of Marko Andrijić whose sons, Petar and Josip, worked on numerous prestigious buildings in Dubrovnik. Flanking the main doorway are lions and some rather lewd naked figures representing Adam and Eve. Above the door sits St Mark, robed as a bishop. Inside, the Cathedral is notable for a splendid, high wooden ceiling; a huge stone canopy, also the work of Andrijić père, and built to his own design; and a richly coloured Tintoretto altarpiece (1550) depicting St Mark flanked by St Bartholomew and St Jerome. In the

south aisle there is an Annunciation that is ascribed to the School of Tintoretto; and in the north aisle is Ivan Meštrović's early 20th-century bronze statue of St Blaise.

To the right of the Cathedral is the **Treasury Museum** ❸ (Opatska Riznica; open summer 10am–1pm, 5–7pm). This elegant limestone building houses an eclectic array: its art works range from 15th-century sacred paintings – including a precious polyptych of *Our Lady of Conception* by Blaž Trogiranin, one of the most respected 15th-century Dalmatian artists – to Ivan Meštrović's 20th-century bronze *Pietà*. There are also ecclesiastical robes, chalices and processional crucifixes; and at ground level there's a cool kitchen, with large metal pots in the hearth and shelves stacked with Roman pots and jars of all shapes and sizes, recovered from the sea in the 1960s.

Directly opposite is another museum worth visiting, the **Town Museum** ❹ (Gradski Muzej; Jan–Mar daily 10am–1pm, Apr–Jun until 2pm, Jul–Sep 9am–9pm, Oct–Dec Mon–Fri 10am–1pm), in a 16th-century Renaissance palace built for the wealthy Gabrielis family. The ground floor has an exhibition on the island's stonemasons; the first floor concentrates on Korčula's second important industry – shipbuilding – which utilised timber from the densely wooded island. At their height, the shipyards rivalled those of Venice and Dubrovnik; at the end of the 18th century there were still 100 shipyards here.

Elsewhere in the museum are rooms housing 17th- to 19th-century furniture,

St Mark's Cathedral   _Tintoretto altarpiece_

elaborate costumes, portraits of the Andrijić family, kitchen implements and, on the top floor, easily overlooked and not mentioned in the museum's guide, photographs of Tito's Partisans.

If you are hungry there are plenty of places to sit down and eat. Korčula's restaurants offer the usual selection of seafood and Dalmatian ham, but they also specialise in pizzas. Try **Buffet-Pizzeria Amfora** south of the Cathedral in Ulica od Teatra for generous pizzas (see ❶). For something fishy, go to **Konoba Adio**

Mare, a short way down Ulica Sveti Roka, which leads into the square from the left, beside the church of St Peter (see ❷). Another of the island's specialities – sea urchin eggs – may prove more difficult to find, unless you know a local fisherman.

THE MARCO POLO EXPERIENCE

It is generally agreed that Marco Polo (1254–1324) was born in Venice, but, as you will soon discover, that is not accepted on this island. Korčula claims the great

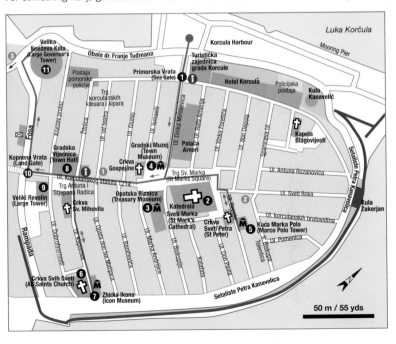

Kopnena Vrata (Land Gate

explorer for its own, believing that he was born here before his family moved to Italy. There is a Hotel Marco Polo (on the next peninsula, east of the Old Town); Marco Polo Tours operate close to the harbour, and you can visit the **Marco Polo Tower** ❺ (open Jul–Aug 9am–9pm, until 3pm Apr– Jun and Sep–Oct) in Ulice Depolo, on the right, off Ulice Sveti Roka. However dubious the associations, it's a lovely place, entered through a vine-covered patio, and with stunning views from the top. The attached building – a graceful, ruined Gothic palace – houses the **Marco Polo Museum** (open daily 10am–7.30pm, http://marcopolo. com.hr), with life-size exhibits re-creating the exploits of the explorer.

In late May there is an annual festival called the Return of Marco Polo, when a suitably clad character is welcomed by the mayor and led to his home, where he entertains the townspeople with stories of his travels, before they all settle down to a concert of Renaissance music.

Korčula is known for its festivals and its desire to keep traditions alive. The major celebration is the Moreška, or Sword Dance Festival, held on St The-odor's Day, 29 July, when medieval knights perform a stylised dance and play. A shortened version of the dance takes place on an outdoor stage in the Ljetno Kino every week in summer.

ICONS AND ICE CREAM

Bypassing the Cathedral, follow the road called Ulica Korčulanskog Statuta 1214.

(The name relates to the City Statute of 1214, one of the oldest Slav legal documents, which laid down the rights and obligations of citizens and regulated trade and agriculture.) At the end of the road, turn left into Ulica Kaporova for **All Saints' Church** ❻ (Svih Svetih; usually open in daylight hours; free) to see a beautiful 15th-century polyptych by Blaž Trogiranin (whose work is also in the Treasury Museum). Next door is the **Icon Museum** ❼ (Zhirka Ikona; open 10am–2pm, 5–7pm), housed in the Hall of the Brotherhood of All Saints. Painted on wood in tempera and gilt, some of the icons are truly moving.

From here, you could follow the broad pine-shaded road (Petra Kanavelića) that leads back around the town in an anti-clock wise direction, stopping for an ice cream at one of the cafés. Alternatively, backtrack to the main road, where it opens out into a small square, with the **Gradska Vijećnica** ❽ (Town Hall) on the right and, on the left, the 15th-century **Veliko Revelin** ❾ (Large Tower), which guards the **Kopnena Vrata** ❿ (Land Gate) to the town.

OUTSIDE THE WALLS

After climbing the tower for far-reaching views of the sea and the coastline, you could go down the steps out of the Old Town and turn right, walking a few metres/yards until you reach the great, cone-shaped **Velika Kneževa Kula** ⓫ (Large Governor's Tower), built at the western corner of the walls to protect both the Governor's Palace and the harbour. Go left here, and fol-

Badija island, off Korčula

low the harbour road for a different view of Korčula and the chance for a swim at one of two small bathing beaches. If you want to check out the Marina, or are going to stay in one of the hotels on the next little peninsula east, go left when you come out of the Land Gate and follow the road round to the right. Here you'll find opportunities for swimming and sailing (Korčula's a truly great place for sailing and hosts a number of regattas) as well as just sitting by the sea, resting your feet and watching the boats in the water.

For one of the most delightful spots for a sundowner, walk about 10 minutes west of the Old Town to the other side of the harbour along Put Svetog Nikole until you reach **Maksimilijan Garden Lounge & Beach Bar** (see ❸). It's also the home of the Memorial Collection of Maksimilijan Vanka, a gallery of paintings by the Croatian painter as well as temporary exhibitions of other Croatian artists.

FURTHER AFIELD

If you plan to stay longer in Korčula and explore some of its beaches, it's about a 15-minute bus ride to the small fishing village of **Lumbarda** to the southeast. Here among the vineyards you'll find several sandy beaches, including the small village beach called Tatinja. The much larger Vela Pržina is tucked into a cove on the southern side of the island. As it's a popular beach it's best to get there early, especially as the bus stops at the beach as well as in the village. Closer to Lumbarda is the equally popular beach at Bilin Zal, which is also connected by bus to Korčula Town as well as taxi boat.

The beach is a favourite spot for sailors to stop for a swim while on excursions around the **Skoji islands** to the north. This archipelago of 19 islands can be visited on day trips from Lumbarda and Korčula Town, and provide an enjoyable escape from the crowds in high season. Trips to the Skoji islands can include discovering hidden beaches, snorkelling, diving, canoeing and kayaking, as well as picnics on the boat.

Food and Drink

❶ BUFFET-PIZZERIA AMFORA

Ulica od Teatra 4; tel: 020-711 739; €
Serves large pizzas, simply grilled fish and good-quality pasta and seafood dishes in an attractive narrow lane.

❷ ADIO MARE

Marka Pola 2; tel: 020-711 253;
www.konobaadiomare.hr; €–€€
Try to get a table on the roof terrace of this atmospheric restaurant with an extensive fish and seafood menu including grilled fish and squid. Booking advised in high season.

❸ MAKSIMILIJAN GARDEN LOUNGE & BEACH BAR

Put Svetog Nikole 39; tel: 091-170 2567;
daily 11am–midnight; €–€€
The top-notch Mediterranean cuisine matches the sunset views at this classy restaurant and lounge overlooking the sea.

DIRECTORY

Hand-picked hotels and restaurants to suit all budgets and tastes, organised by area, plus select nightlife listings, an alphabetical listing of practical information, a language guide and an overview of the best books and films to give you a flavour of the city.

Sleep in style at Stari Grad

ACCOMMODATION

Many of Dubrovnik's hotels are spacious, modern and efficient, with air conditioning, swimming pools, room service, etc. A large number of has been swallowed up by a small number of conglomerates such as Adriatic Luxury Hotels. Many visitors to Dubrovnik come on package deals, which usually include half-board accommodation, generally at a price considerably lower than the rack rates given below. Hotel rates are often quoted in euros, but charged in kuna.

There are a few smaller, more personal hotels, however, and a growing number of rooms and apartments for rent – look for signs saying *sobe* or *apartman*. The identical dark blue signs indicate that the establishment is regulated. A room in a private house usually doesn't include breakfast, so you have to go to the nearest café.

All hotel rates vary according to the time of year – there are some very good deals to be had off-season. The rates below are for a standard, en suite double room in high season (July–mid-September) including breakfast.

Price categories (for a double room in high season including breakfast):
€€€€ = over 2,000kn
€€€ = 1,000–1,999kn
€€ = 500–999kn
€ = under 500kn

Old Town

Amoret Apartments
4 locations; tel: 914-050 508;
www.dubrovnik-amoret.com
Choose from 15 apartments set in four former palaces near the cathedral, all furnished with antiques and family heirlooms. The one-bedroom flats have full kitchens, but if you don't plan to cook much, the studio flats with small kitchenettes are a good budget option. €€–€€€

Family House Fascination
Domino 8; tel: 020-323 112;
www.fascination-dubrovnik.com
There's a choice of three apartments in this 18th-century stone house in a narrow street leading up from Stradun. All guests can use the garden and a delightful terrace. €€€

Fresh Sheets
Bunićeva Poljana 6; tel: 091-896 7509;
www.freshsheetsbedandbreakfast.com
Croatian-Canadian couple Jon and Sanja run this friendly B&B next to the cathedral in the old town, with smartly furnished modern rooms and bathrooms. This is the place to come for the personal touch, including copious made-to-order breakfasts. €€€

Smartly decorated room at Stari Grad

Karmen Apartments

Bandureva 1; tel: 020-323 433; 098 619 282; www.karmendu.com

These three spacious and one smaller apartment are in a family house right beside the harbour. They're attractively decorated, with bright rugs and bedspreads, original paintings on the walls and smart, modern bathrooms. The friendly, helpful hosts have loads of local knowledge that they are happy to share. €€–€€€

Prijeko Palace

Prijeko 22; tel: 020-321 145; www.prijekopalace.com

Contemporary artists have been let loose on the nine luxurious rooms in this 16th-century house in Prijeko, and furnished them with exquisite original works. The result is a riot of colour and a sumptuous baroque style that's a world away from modern minimalism. Head to the roof terrace for fantastic views of the Old Town. €€€–€€€€

Pucić Palace

Od Puča 1; Tel: 020-326 222; www.thepucicpalace.com

This is the last word in discreet luxury and comfort. Set in a Renaissance palace, it offers 19 rooms and suites. There's a restaurant, a brasserie, a beauty centre and a library in an old chapel. The hotel also has a private yacht, available (separate charge) for trips up the coast. €€€€

St Joseph's

Svetog Josipa 3, tel: 020-432 089; www.stjosephs.hr

One of the old town's newest additions is this elegant and intimate boutique hotel in a 500-year-old house tucked away in a quiet lane off Stradun. Its stylish six rooms are decorated in a refined yet relaxed French country cottage style and come with kitchenettes and modern marble bathrooms. €€€€

Stari Grad

Od Sigurate 4; tel: 020-322 244; www.hotelstarigrad.com

This eight-room boutique hotel occupies an aristocratic family house just off Stradun. Smartly furnished modern rooms have contemporary decor, and the rooftop terrace restaurant has wonderful views of the old town. €€€€

Villa Ragusa

Zudioska 15; tel: 098-765 634; www.villaragusadubrovnik.com

It's a bit of a climb to reach this 600-year-old building, but it's worth it if you want a comfortable budget option. There's a nicely rustic room on each of the five floors, with a shared kitchen and dining area. The whole house is also available to rent. €–€€

Ploče

Hotel Excelsior

Frana Supila 12; tel: 020-353 000; www.adriaticluxuryhotels.com

Cliff-top Villa Dubrovnik

About five minutes' walk from the Ploče Gate is this large five-star hotel with splendid views of the old town. The hotel dates from 1913 but has a thoroughly contemporary interior, along with an outdoor and indoor pool and well-equipped spa. €€€€

Grand Villa Argentina
Frana Supila 14; tel: 020-440 555;
www.adriaticluxuryhotels.com
This hotel amid pine and palm trees is in a beautiful setting about five minutes' walk from Ploče Gate, overlooking the sea, with views of Lokrum and the old town. There's a private beach, indoor and outdoor pools, sauna, gym and an attractive restaurant terrace. €€€€

Villa Dubrovnik
Vlaha Bukovca 6; tel: 020-500 300;
www.villa-dubrovnik.hr
The setting is incomparable in this cliff-top hotel with an indoor/outdoor pool and a private beach. This rooftop bar of this stylish member of the Small Luxury Hotels of the World has some of the city's best views. €€€€

Villa Odak
Frana Supila 16; www.villa-odak.
dubrovnikhotelscroatia.net
One of the best budget options in Ploče has functionally furnished rooms with kitchenettes and a shared terrace with great views of the Old Town. It's also handy for beaches, as it's between Banje and Sveti Jakov beaches. €–€€

Villa Orsula
Frana Supila 14; tel: 020-440 588;
www.adriaticluxuryhotels.com
Thirteen luxurious rooms are behind the 1939 stone façade of this attractive stone-built boutique hotel. Lush gardens cascade down to the sea and the hotel's private beach. Many of the contemporary rooms have sea views and private balconies. €€€€

Pile

Hotel Bellevue
Pera čingrije 7; tel: 020-330 000;
www.adriaticluxuryhotels.com
Carved into a cliff is this luxurious hotel built overlooking Miramare Bay. Each of the 93 rooms has a sea view. Lots of local wood and stone have been used in the design, and rooms feature paintings by prestigious Croatian artists. €€€€

Hilton Imperial Hotel
Marijana Blažića 2; tel: 020-320 320;
www.hilton.com
Two 19th-century buildings make this newly refurbished hotel fronting on to Branitelja Dubrovnika, the road leading uphill from the Pile Gate. Wood and marble finishes give a luxurious air, and many of the rooms have sea views and balconies. There's a large terrace, restaurant, piano bar, indoor pool and gym. €€€€

Room with a view   *Jacuzzi on the terrace, Villa Dubrovnik*

Hotel Lero

Iva Vojnovića 14; tel: 020-341 4353;
www.hotel-lero.hr

On the main road between Pile and Lapad, the Lero is a rather dull block of a hotel, but it has a good location, approximately 200 metres/yards from the beach. There's also an outdoor pool and a wellness centre. €€–€€€

Gruž

Hotel Lapad

Lapadska Obala 37; tel: 020-455 555;
www.hotel-lapad.hr

This attractive 19th-century building with a modern wing is on the Lapad side of Gruž Harbour, 3km (2 miles) from the Pile Gate and on a bus route. Rooms in the new wing have air conditioning. There's a pool and a boat service to the nearest beach in summer. €€€

Hotel Petka

Obala Stjepana Radića 38; tel: 020-410 500; www.hotelpetka.hr

Close to the ferry port, this functional hotel is good value. Get a room with a harbour view and balcony if you can. It's also on a regular bus route into the old town. €€

Lapad

Hotel Dubrovnik

Šetalište Kralje Zvonimira bb; tel: 020-435 030; www.hoteldubrovnik.hr

This friendly, no-frills hotel is on a popular pedestrianised street just a few minutes' walk from the beach. Its 22 en suite rooms and four suites all have air conditioning and balconies as well as free WiFi. €€

Hotel Dubrovnik Palace

Masarykov put 20; tel: 020-430 000;
www.adriaticluxuryhotels.com

Set into the cliff below pine woods, the Hotel Dubrovnik Palace dominates the Lapad headland. All the 307 rooms have sea views and balconies and the ground-floor bar (one of several) has a wall of glass directly over the sea. There are four pools, a private beach and a diving centre. €€€€

Hotel Komodor

Masarykov put 5; tel: 020-433 673;
www.dubrovnikhotels.travel

This is the first in the row of five hotels in this street along the side of Lapad Bay, all of which are part of the Maestral chain. It is the oldest and most traditional of the five, and has a restaurant and outdoor pool. €€

Hotel Kompas

Kardinala Stepinca 21; tel: 020-299 000;
www.adriaticluxuryhotels.com

After a complete reconstruction, the Kompas reopened in 2015 as a sleek four-star that fronts on to Lapad Bay. It's smart and modern, with indoor and outdoor pools, a spa and several bars and restaurants. €€€€

Rixos Libertas Dubrovnik

Liechtensteinov put 3; tel: 021-770 620;

Exclusive Villa Elita at the Importanne Resort

http://libertasdubrovnik.rixos.com

This sprawling Seventies hotel hugs the cliff overlooking the bay between Lapad and the old town. Contemporary rooms come with balconies, and the restaurants offer Turkish and Italian cuisine. It's also home to Dubrovnik's only casino, and the views from the pool are magnificent. €€€€

Hotel Splendid

Masarykov put 10; tel: 020-433 633; www.dubrovnikhotels.travel

Another in the Maestral chain, the Splendid backs straight on to the beach and bay. It's somewhat impersonal but comfortable and efficient, and many rooms have balconies and sea views €€–€€€

Hotel Uvala

Masarykov put 10; tel: 020-433 608; www.dubrovnikhotels.travel

Although its exterior is quite plain, the Uvala is the smartest of the five Maestral Lapad hotels. Sea view rooms have minimalist decor, and there's a well-designed wellness centre with indoor and outdoor pools. €€€

Hotel Vis

Masarykov put 4; tel: 020-433 605; www.dubrovnikhotels.travel

The rooms are functional but the hotel's location, restaurant terrace and beach make up for the simply furnished interiors. It's worth upgrading to a sea view with a balcony. €€–€€€

Vila Mičika

Mata Vodopića 10; tel: 020-437 332; www.vilamicika.hr

Rooms are very basic but it's a good choice for those on a budget who want to be near Lapad's beaches. At least the rooms have their own bathrooms, and for the price it's hard to quibble when you get free WiFi and the use of a microwave and fridge. €

Villa Wolff

Nika i Meda Pučića 1; tel: 020-438 710; http://villa-wolff.hr

A 10-minute drive from the old town leads to this romantic hotel with stunning views across the bay and a pleasant palm tree-shaded terrace on which to have breakfast. There's no pool, but there's safe swimming from the rocks immediately below. €€€

Hotel Zagreb

Šetalište Kralje Zvonimira 27; tel: 020-438 930

This comfortable, traditional hotel is in an attractive terracotta-coloured building set in palm-shaded gardens. Its dining room has a glassed-in terrace. It's less than five minutes' walk from the beach and about two minutes' walk from a bus stop. €€€

Babin Kuk

Hotel Argosy

Iva Dulčića 41; tel: 020-446 100; www.valamar.com

This modern four-star hotel sits in large

Suite at Villa Elita   *Spacious bathroom at Villa Elita*

landscaped gardens with an infinity pool. Many of the contemporary rooms have sea-facing balconies, and the wellness centre includes a fresh-water indoor pool. Cava Beach is about 200 metres/yards away. €€€

Dubrovnik President

Iva Dulčića 142; tel: 020-441 100;
www.valamar.com

This large hotel commands the headland, facing out to sea like a great ship. All rooms have balconies and sea views, and there are tennis courts and a gym among its amenities. External lifts take guests down to the hotel's rocky beaches (the other hotels in the Valamar complex include the Valamar Club and the Valamar Lacroma Resort; see website above for details.). €€€€

Importanne Resort

Kardinala Stepinca 31; tel: 020-440 100;
www.importanneresort.com

The other major player on the Babin Kuk peninsula, this group includes the Neptun, the Ariston, Importanne Suites and the Villa Elita – extremely elite and expensive. The Neptun has a restaurant/café terrace that offers one of the best places in Dubrovnik to watch the sun go down (see website above for details). €€€–€€€€

Hotel More

Kardinala Stepinca 33; tel: 020-494 200;
www.hotel-more.hr

In a prime position overlooking Lapad Bay is this classy and understated five-star hotel. Try to get a room with a balcony and sea view, but all come with whirlpool baths. The funky Cave Bar, with its dramatic cave-like interior, has become a popular hangout for guests and locals alike. €€€€

Tirena Hotel

Iva Dulčića 36; tel: 020-445 100;
www.valamar.com

Straightforward rooms and plenty of family facilities make up this dependable three-star close to Cava Beach. The decor is simple, but most rooms have balconies, and there's an outdoor pool plus a separate one for children. €€€

Orašac

Sun Gardens

Na Moru 1; tel: 020-361 500;
www.dubrovniksungardens.com

It's unabashed luxury at this contemporary, cliff-hugging resort 11km (7 miles) west of Dubrovnik, with an enormous spa, infinity pool and its own marina. During the season, a boat shuttles guests to the old town. €€€€

Cavtat

Hotel Croatia

Frankopanska 10; tel: 020-475 555;
www.adriaticluxuryhotels.com

On a peninsula to the south of the village is this big, modern hotel that's pop-

ular with tour agencies. There's sailing, a large pool, children's activities and great views, but it's a bit of a hike down to the beach. €€€

Hotel Epidaurus
Od Zala; tel: 051-710 444;
www.remisens.com
The sister hotel to the Albatros (see below) is a no-fills affair that is redeemed by its location by the beach. Simple rooms have balconies, and there's also an outdoor pool. €€

Remisens Family Hotel Albatros
Od Žala 1; tel: 051-710 444;
www.remisens.com
This sprawling modern hotel is a family-friendly place right by the beach. Rooms are functionally furnished but come with balconies, and there are indoor and outdoor pools. Although it calls itself an all-inclusive hotel, you can stay on a B&B basis. €€€

Hotel Supetar
Ante Starčevića 27; tel: 020-479 833;
www.adriaticluxuryhotels.com
A comfortable hotel in a traditional stone building right by the bay, the Supetar has 28 rooms, a restaurant, bar and breakfast terrace with wonderful views, as well as friendly staff. €€€

Villa Pattiera
Trumbićev put 9; tel: 020-478 800;
www.villa-pattiera.hr

The birthplace of the Croatian tenor Tino Pattiera is a cosy four-star hotel by the harbour. All 12 rooms have either a shared or private terrace or balcony, and the hotel also runs the Dalmacija restaurant across the road. €€€

Koločep

Kalamota Island Resort
Donje Čelo 45; tel: 020-312 150;
www.kalamotaislandresort.com
What had been the Hotel Villas Koločep has been turned into an adults-only all-inclusive resort overlooking Donje Čelo Bay. Modern rooms come with balconies or terraces, and there's a pool if you want a change from the beach in front of the resort. €€€€

Šipan

Hotel Božica
Suđurađ 3; tel: 020-325 400; www.hotel-bozica.hr
This intimate four-star is only about 15 metres/yards from the sea and comes with its own beach and mooring for yachts. You'll want one of its sea-facing rooms with a balcony to enjoy splendid views. There's also an outdoor pool and a particularly good restaurant. €€€€

Lopud

Hotel Glavović
Obala Iva Kuljevana bb; tel: 020-759 359;
www.hotel-glavovic.hr

Majestic Korčula at sunrise

The rooms have simple furnishings, but this friendly family-run hotel is in a great location right on the harbourside. It has a good restaurant, and the beach is practically at your feet. €–€€

Hotel Lafodia

Obala Ive Kuljevana 51; tel: 020-450 300; www.lafodiahotel.com

This ultra-modern hotel near the harbour rises up like twin cruise ships divided by cascading café terraces and gardens and topped with a spa. Contemporary rooms are sleek and enhanced by balconies with wonderful sea views and a private beach. €€€–€€€€

Hotel Villa Vilina

Obala Iva Kuljevana 5; tel: 020-759 333; www.villa-vilina.hr

In a historic, four-star family house by the harbour, the Vilina has 15 rooms and three suites, an outdoor pool and an excellent restaurant that includes fruit and olives from the garden on its menu. €€€

Mljet

Hotel Odisej

Pomena; 020-362 111; www.adriaticluxuryhotels.com

Parkland surrounds this large modern hotel overlooking Pomena bay in the Mljet National Park. Ask for a room with a balcony to make up for the somewhat bland decor, some of which needs refreshing. €€–€€€

Korčula

Hotel Korčula

Šetalište Frana Kršinića 102; tel: 020-711 078; www.hotelkorcula.com

This elegant Korčula hotel, right by the harbour, has 22 rooms, a lovely vine-shaded terrace, a good restaurant and wood panelled public areas. Rooms can be small but the location is excellent. €€€

Lešić Dimitri Palace

Don Pavla Poše 1–6; tel: 020-715 560; www.ldpalace.com

Set in an 18th-century bishop's palace in the heart of the old town is this chic boutique hotel and Relais & Châteaux member. Its opulent rooms hark back to the days of the Silk Road, with suitably oriental touches. €€€€

Mali Ston

Hotel Vila Koruna

Pelješki put 1; tel: 020-754 999; www.vila-koruna.hr

Famous as Mali Ston's oldest restaurant and purveyor of local oysters, the Vila Koruna has comfortable, functional rooms and a pleasant indoor restaurant as well as the large glass terrace overlooking the bay. €€

Above 5 Rooftop Restaurant lives up to its name

RESTAURANTS

Eating out in Dubrovnik is a delight, especially during the summer, when nearly all restaurants have outside tables, either on a terrace, a pavement, or right beside the sea. It does help, however, if you like seafood. Meat does feature but fishy things predominate – as you would expect in a city on the shores of the Adriatic. Anyone familiar with Italian food will notice many similarities. You will also see a degree of similarity in Dubrovnik's restaurant menus: from the economical to the expensive, they all feature similar dishes, although the standard of cooking and presentation vary a great deal. Menus are invariably translated into English, and often into German and French as well.

While some establishments are called restaurants, others are known as a *konoba*. A *konoba* was originally a kind of taverna, a somewhat humble or rustic place to eat, and in the rural regions this is still the case, but in the city the two words are interchangeable. You may find a relatively expensive restaurant calling itself a *konoba*, while a more basic one is known as a restaurant.

Local people usually eat lunch around 1.30pm and dinner at about 9pm, but restaurateurs are so used to catering to foreign visitors, who provide most of their trade, that they will serve lunch from midday throughout most of the afternoon, and dinner from round 6pm. At the height of the season, many restaurants carry on serving dinner until about 11pm.

Some restaurants impose a cover charge per person, typically 20 kuna each. This should be made clear on the menu before you order. If you want tap water rather than bottled water, ask for "*obična* (obeechna) *voda*". Ordering fish by the kilo can be an expensive business, so make certain you and the waiter know how much you've ordered and what the price will be.

As in many tourist hot spots, Dubrovnik has its share of restaurants whose staff tout for business in Stradun during meal times. As the city also has its share of mediocre restaurants, don't feel compelled to pay attention to the touts. They'll soon get bored and move on to someone else.

Approximate prices are based on a two-course meal for one, with a bottle of house wine.
€ = under 300 kn
€€ = 300–500 kn
€€€ = over 500 kn

Old Town

360°
Svetog Dominika, tel: 020-322 222; www.360dubrovnik.com

Lamb dish at Above 5 Rooftop

A medieval arsenal set in the City Walls is the setting for this sophisticated restaurant with fantastic views of the Old Port. They don't skimp on top-class ingredients here: turbot, venison, lobster and the ubiquitous truffle feature on a Mediterranean menu. It's a magnet in the season, so book ahead. Closed in winter and Mondays. Dinner only. €€€

Above 5 Rooftop Restaurant
Od Sigurate 4; tel: 020-322 244; www.hotelstarigrad.com

Once you've climbed up about five flights of stairs, you're rewarded with one of the most romantic views of Dubrovnik's old town. The rooftop restaurant at Hotel Stari Grad is tiny and it's worth reserving a table for beautifully cooked Mediterranean cuisine. €€–€€€

Azur
Pobijana 10; tel: 020-324 806; www.azurvision.com

Croatia meets Asia in this laid-back little restaurant tucked away near the city walls not far from the Aquarium. The innovative menu is heavy on curry, Japanese and Thai spices livening up chicken, beef and fish dishes in relaxed, newly refurbished surroundings. €

Barba
Boškovićeva 5; tel: 091-205 3488

Between Prijeko and Stradun is this unpretentious little seafood café with a casually rustic interior – just the spot for a quick but delicious lunch. Try the octopus burger or tempura prawns. €

La Capella
Pucić Palace Hotel; Od Puča 1; tel: 020-326 222; www.thepucic palace.com

This roof-terrace restaurant is smart without being stuffy, and has lovely views over the old town. Some dishes have a Middle Eastern flavour, and there is also plenty of fish, including lobster with black risotto. €€€

Dalmatino
Miha Pracata 6; tel: 020-327 404; www.dalmatino-dubrovnik.com

This cosy restaurant in one of the old town's narrow streets also features an intimate courtyard. Fresh seafood and meat dishes have clean Mediterranean flavours and include black ink risotto, truffle pasta and lobster fettucine. €

Steak House Domino
Od Domina 3; tel: 020-323 103; www.steakhousedomino.com

Domino, close to the church of the same name, has been going for years and provides good-value meals on a terrace in a small square. Along with the steaks it has plenty of seafood dishes. €€

Pavement tables at Proto

Gil's Little Bistro

Petilovrijenci 4, tel: 020-321 168; www. gils.hr

Meat-lovers flock to this tiny, lively bistro in a narrow side street off Stradun. You choose your cut and it's weighed and priced in front of you to save any nasty surprises at the end of the meal. €€

Kamenice

Gundulićeva Poljana 8; tel: 020-323 682

Tables spread out in front of this long-established restaurant where fish figures prominently on the menu. The grilled squid is particularly good, and they also specialise in oysters, after which the restaurant is named. €–€€

Lady PiPi

Antuninska 23; tel: 020-321 154

Don't let the name put you off this appealing place in the shadow of the city walls north of Prijeko. Meat dishes are cooked in front of you on the open barbecue under the vine-covered terrace, and a higher terrace gives you great views of the old town. €

Lokanda Peskarija

Na Ponti (Old Port) bb; tel: 020-324 750; www.mea-culpa.hr

Open from 8am until midnight in summer, this small, efficient place with tables sprawling towards the Old Port jetty has a very short menu. It's mainly fish and seafood, brought to the table in sizzling, blackened pots, accompanied by carafes of house wine and large, no-nonsense salads. €

Lucin Kantun

Od Sigurate 4a; tel: 020-321 003

Just off Stradun is this pleasant, unpretentious little place with friendly staff and an open kitchen. The restaurant makes good use of locally grown vegetables and serves some excellent tapas dishes. €€

Mea Culpa

Za Rokom 3; tel: 020-323 430; www.meaculpa-pizzeria.com

The biggest pizzas in town served at wooden benches in a narrow street parallel to Stradun. Don't be afraid to ask for one to share – they are large enough. Resist the pleading eyes of the resident cats if you are strong-minded enough. €

Nishta

Prijeko bb, tel: 020-322 088; www.nishtarestaurant.com

True vegetarian food is hard to come by in Croatia, so it's not surprising that this small restaurant on the corner of Prijeko and Palmotićeva has a devoted following. Asian, Middle Eastern and Mexican flavours mingle with local dishes, and there are vegan and gluten-free options. €

Oliva Pizzeria

Lučarica 5; tel: 020-324 594

Proto's popular upstairs terrace

Presentation is key at Proto

In a narrow lane behind St Blaise Church is this lively pizzeria, where they serve a large selection of good-value pizzas along with more basic pasta dishes and salads. €

Oyster Bar & Sushi Bota

Od Pustijerne bb, tel: 020-324 034; www.bota-sare.hr

Oysters from Ston are given the Japanese treatment in this sleek modern restaurant by the Cathedral. In fact, most of the Adriatic fruits of the sea are beautifully turned into sushi, teriyaki and tempura delights. €–€€

Poklisar

Od Ribarnice 1 (Old Port); tel: 020-322 176; www.poklisar.com

Pizzas and fish dishes are served in a cheerful atmosphere beside the harbour, where at lunchtime you can watch competing vendors of boat trips plying for trade. They also have a separate sushi menu, as well as one for children. There's live music some evenings, and it seems to keep going until around midnight if there are customers. €€

Presa

Djordjiceva 2; tel: 989 892 942

Known for its grilled beef burgers and toasted sandwiches with flatbread and/or chips, this tiny bar is one of the most budget-friendly and tasty options in the touristy Old Town. For dessert, try the delicious pancakes. €

Proto

Široka 1; tel: 020-323 234; www.esculaprestaurants.com

Established in 1886 and still going strong, Proto, just off Stradun at the Pile Gate end, serves reliably good meat and fish at pavement tables, indoors or (most popular) on an upstairs terrace. Recommended by the Michelin guide, so book ahead in high season. €€€

Ribar

Kneza Damjana Jude; tel: 020-323 194

A friendly place, close to the Aquarium, the Ribar has been run by the Kovačić family for years. They specialise in fish, but there are also good meat dishes on offer. One of their specialities is *topla marenda*, a late-morning mezze-like selection of warm snacks. €

Rozario

Prijeko 1; tel: 020-322 015; www.konoba-rozario.hr

One of the best of the Prijeko restaurants is close to the Dominican monastery and serves excellent Dalmatian food in a cosy dining room or at a few tables in a shady corner outside. As it's not very big, it's a good idea to book. Lunch and dinner daily. Closed in January. €€

Spaghetteria Toni

Božidarevićeva 14; tel: 020-323 134; www.spaghetteria-toni.com

Superb presentation at Mimoza

Just off Puča, this is the place for large helpings of inexpensive and very well cooked homemade pasta, served with a wide variety of sauces. Open daily 11am–11pm. €

Stara Loza

Prijeko 22, tel: 020-321 145;
www.prijekopalace.com

The restaurant on the ground floor of the Prijeko Palace is as classy as the hotel itself. They do an imaginative take on local cuisine and add a few international dishes. The oxtail starter and suckling pig main course are stand-out dishes. €€

Taj Mahal

Nikole Gučetića 2; tel: 020-323 221;
www.tajmahal-dubrovnik.com

Get a taste of neighbouring Bosnia in this cave-like restaurant decorated in Ottoman style. Dishes include Bosnian staples such as *ćevapčići*, spicy meat rissoles and savoury pastries known as *burek*, filled with meat or cheese. There's another branch in Hotel Lero. €

Wanda

Prijeko 8, tel: 098-944 9317;
www.wandarestaurant.com

The influence is very Italian in this cosy restaurant whose quality of food makes it stand out from many of its Prijeko competitors. Try the giant grilled prawns or the lobster spaghetti. €€

Ploče

Gusta Me

Hvarska bb; tel: 020-420 013;
www.gustame-dubrovnik.com

You get lovely views of the old port in this buzzing restaurant just outside the Ploče Gate. Good-value meat and seafood dishes are served on a large sheltered terrace, and it's worth booking ahead during high season. Open daily 10am–midnight. €€

Konoba Komarda

Frana Supila 6a; tel: 091-720 8876

If only the food were as good as the views of the Old Port from this waterside restaurant. It's not, however, but it's worth stopping here if you're in need of a coffee and maybe some *palačinke* (crêpes). €€

Revelin Club

Sv. Dominika bb; tel: 020-436 010;
www.clubrevelin.com

The Revelin is better known for its cavernous disco inside this medieval fort overlooking the Old Port. But its outdoor restaurant under giant trees comes with glorious views and decent Italian-influenced meat and seafood dishes. €€

Pile

Dubravka 1836

Brsalje 1; tel: 020-426 319; www.nautika restaurants.com/dubravka-restaurant-cafe

Just outside the Pile Gate and overlooking Fort Lovrijenac, Dubravka's

Harbourfront restaurant

Straight from the grill at Mimoza

large terrace gives diners some of the views in town. The varied menu offers generous pizzas and pastas as well as salads, fresh fish and meat dishes. The cocktails are worth checking out. €–€€

Mimoza

Branitelja Dubrovnika 9; tel: 020-411 157; www.restaurant-mimoza-dubrovnik.com/
Dalmatian meat and seafood specialities are served in this large airy dining room and terrace a few minutes' walk from Pile. They also feature meat and fish dishes cooked *ispod peke*, under a cast-iron dome that keeps everything succulent. €€

Nautika

Brsalje 3, tel: 020- 442 526; www.nautikarestaurants.com
This Dubrovnik institution had been hosting the great and the good for decades, serving top-class seafood by the water's edge just outside the Pile Gate. Its beautiful setting offers amazing views over Lovrijenac and Bokar forts. €€€

Posat

Uz Posat 1 (just outside Pile Gate); tel: 020-421 194; www.posat-dubrovnik.com
The setting, fronting a car park, is unprepossessing, but once you are settled on the upper terrace your view is over Fort Lovrijenac. The home-cooked food is good, especially some innovative lobster and cod dishes. Daily 8am–midnight. €€

Sesame

Dante Alighieria 2; tel: 020-412 910; www.sesame.hr
This pleasant little restaurant serving good risottos and homemade pasta dishes is in a narrow street off the main Ante Starčevića road leading west from Pile Gate. It's popular with students, as one of the university faculties is nearby. It also has basic rooms for rent. €

Mount Srđ

Panorama

Upper Cable Car Station, Mount Srđ; tel: 020-312 664; www.dubrovnikcablecar. com
The views are incomparable in this restaurant at the top of the cable car station. And the food, if a little pricey, is worthy of the trip up to Mount Srđ either via cable car or the 90-minute hike. It's a good stop for lunch or to catch the sunset. €–€€

Gruž

Blidinje

Lapadska Obala 21; tel: 020-358 794; http://konoba-blidinje.com
Good-value pizzeria that also does slow-cooked meat dishes *ispod peke* – under an iron bell. These should be ordered a couple of hours in advance, and try to get a table on the upstairs terrace with views of the harbour. €

Restaurant Orsan

Ivana Zajca 2; tel: 020-436 822;

Local wines

www.restaurant-orsan-dubrovnik.com
Slightly further up the harbourside on the bay, the Orsan (the name means boathouse) serves the good-quality fish, meat and rice dishes. It's right on the jetty in a lively setting, with views of all the action on the harbour. €€

Taverna Otto

Nikole Tesle 8; tel: 095- 848 4316;
www.tavernaotto.com

Strong Mediterranean flavours can be savoured in an atmospheric stone vaulted room or outside on the pleasant terrace. Tuna with white bean purée and olive tapenade join hearty meat dishes such as braised lamb shanks. €€

Porat

Obala Stjepana Radica no.30; tel: 020 333 552; www.porat-dubrovnik.com

Porat takes full advantage of its harbour location and the fishing boats docking in front of the restaurant with their daily catch of fish, crabs and other seafood. Another speciality is steak – cooked to perfection. €€

Lapad and Babin Kuk

Despite the number of hotels on these two peninsulas, there are relatively few restaurants. This may be because many hotels provide half-board accommodation, and most visitors don't venture outside to eat.

Restaurant Casa

Nika i Meda Pucića 1; tel: 020-438 710;

http://villa-wolff.hr/restaurant-casa
The restaurant at the Villa Wolff is in an enviable setting right on Lapad Bay. The menu changes with the seasons but will always include fresh fish and seafood and Dalmatian specialities. Open daily breakfast, lunch and dinner. €€

Eden

Kardinala Stepinca 54; tel: 020-435 133;

Lovely views of Lapad Bay come with this friendly restaurant with a vine-covered roof terrace. Seafood pasta and risotto dishes are good value and served without fuss. €

Komin

Iva Dulčića 136; tel: 020-435 636;
www.restaurant-komin.com

Unless you are staying in one of the Babin Kuk hotels, you are unlikely to stumble across this place, but it's close to the terminus of the No.6 bus. Set in a family-oriented little park with a large terrace, it specialises in grilled meat and fish. €–€€

Konoba Konavoka

Šetaliste Kralja Zvonimira 38; tel: 020-435 105

The fishing-tackle motif on the covered terrace may be a bit overdone in this informal restaurant on the pedestrianised street leading to Lapad Bay. But the food is good (especially the seafood risotto), and the service is prompt and friendly. €–€€

The view at Restaurant Zoë   *A simple dish of anchovies*

Levanat

Nika i Meda Pucića 15; tel: 020-435 352;
www.restaurant-levanat.com

Follow the seaside path from Restaurant Casa and you will come to this delightful place. Prawns in honey with sage and salmon carpaccio are among the more unusual dishes, but standards such as stuffed squid and mussel *bouzzara* (in white wine and garlic) are excellent, too. Or you can just have a drink and watch the sun set over the sea. €€€

Restaurant Pantarul

Kralja Tomislava 1; tel: 020-333 486,
www.pantarul.com

There are a few Asian touches to the mainly Dalmatian menu in this friendly restaurant with contemporary interiors. Well-crafted dishes include venison stew and grilled prawns wrapped in sole, and the five-course fish and meat tasting menus are particularly good value. Closed Mon. €–€€

Shizuku Japanese Cuisine

Kneza Domagoja 1; tel: 020-311 493

If you're in the mood for a change from Croatian cuisine, then try these plates of sushi, tempura and other classic Japanese dishes. It gets very busy in the summer, so it's best to book ahead – especially if you want a table outside on the terrace. €–€€

Restaurant Zoë

Kardinala Stepinca 31; tel: 020-440 100;
www.importanneresort.com

Stupendous views of the bay go a long way to make up for a somewhat limited menu. Fresh seafood is the star, of course, with octopus and grilled sardines among the stand-outs. €€

Lopud

Restoran Glavović

Obala Iva Kuljevana bb; tel: 020-759 359;
www.hotel-glavovic.hr

This family-run hotel restaurant is located right on the harbourside, offering wonderful views to go with good-quality seafood dishes. It's not the cheapest place in town, but the setting makes up for it. €€–€€€

Konoba Peggy

Narikla 22; tel: 020-759 036; www.pavlovic-pension-lopud.com

Just a few metres from the harbour, this is a popular spot with a large leafy terrace and substantial helpings of fish and seafood. It can get busy, as day-trippers are often pointed in this direction and may arrive in a bunch. €

Obala

Obala Iva Kuljevana 18; tel: 020-759 170;
www.obalalopud.com

There are tables so close to the water you could almost dip your toes in as you eat. There is also a covered terrace and an indoor dining area. Fish couldn't be fresher and the salads are great too, especially when washed down with local wine. €€

Koločep

Villa Ruža

Donje Čelo; tel: 098-443 382; www.villa-ruza.com

The setting is sublime in this 1930s stone villa in a pine-shaded garden at the far end of the seaside promenade. If you can take your eyes off the sea views, tuck into seafood risottos or whatever the fishermen have brought in that day. €€

Cavtat

Bougenvila

Obala Ante Starčevića 9, tel: 020-479 949; www.bugenvila.eu

Classic Dalmatian cooking is given a modern touch in this smart harbourside restaurant with friendly service. Seafood-lovers can indulge in butter-poached lobster or monkfish with clams, while carnivores can try the rib-eye steak with sweetbreads. €€

Dalmacija

Trumbićev put 9; tel: 020-478 800; www.villa-pattiera.hr

Set in a busy little triangle at the southern end of the harbour promenade, this popular place has been in business since 1979. As you would expect from the name, it offers Dalmatian cooking, mainly fish but also good meat dishes, and is usually bustling at lunchtime. €€

Konoba Ivan

Tiha put 5; tel: 020-790 002

On the other side of the peninsula (but only a few hundred metres if you go across the narrow neck), Konoba Ivan is a small, cheerful place right by the water's edge where fresh fish and grilled meat, accompanied by carafes of house wine, make a good lunch. €

Caffe Bar Zino

Obala Ante Starčevića 5, tel: 020-478 300; www.zino-cavtat.com

This cheap and cheerful spot by the harbour has a simple menu of pizzas, sandwiches and snacks, but it's immensely good value. The portions are almost embarrassingly huge: you'll need a hearty appetite to finish a pizza on your own. Even the sandwiches are enormous. €

Mljet

Konoba Galija

Pomena 7, Pomena; tel: 020-744 029

One of a string of little restaurants along Pomena's harbourside (facing the Hotel Odisej across the bay), Galicija has tables in a leafy arbour and live lobsters swimming in a huge tank. Portions are generous, so feel free to share. €

Melita

Sveta Marija; tel: 020-744 145; www.mljet-restoranmelita.com

There's a bit of a trade-off in this restaurant in the remains of the monastery on St Mary's Island. The setting is astounding, but the food can be hit and miss. Simple lunch dishes are your best bet. If you are staying overnight on the island and want dinner, you should book. €€

Cavtat's waterfront is lined with restaurants

Stella Maris

Polače 22, Polače; tel: 098-619 287

Another Polače restaurant with a harbourfront site, this one so close to the ferry dock that you could sit here until the gangplank is about to go up. It offers the usual seafood and grilled meat dishes along with local wine and friendly service. €€

Restoran Stermasi

Saplunara; tel: 098-939 0362;
www.stermasi.hr

Set on a hillside overlooking the rocky bay is this friendly restaurant that specialises in dishes cooked *ispod peke* – under a cast-iron bell. Allow a couple of hours if you order one – or order it in advance – as it's the epitome of slow cooking. There's even a vegetarian option, which is a rarity here. €€–€€€

Korčula

Hotel Korčula

Obala Dr Franje Tudjmana bb;
tel: 020-711 078;
www.hotelkorcula.com

The hotel restaurant has an elegant dining room and a pretty vine-covered terrace opposite the ferry dock. There's an extensive list of local wines to accompany the excellent fish dishes. €€–€€€

Filippi

Šetalište Petra Kanavelića; tel: 020-711 690

Boasting beautiful sea views, this fine restaurant serves excellent seafood and home-made pasta dishes. Leave space for the delicious desserts and the wine selection doesn't disappoint either. €€€

Mali Ston

All the restaurants in little Mali Ston specialise in the oysters and mussels that are cultivated here, and of which they are very proud. They are the reason people flock here for Sunday lunch, but the venues also serve a range of other seafood and fish, and some meat dishes.

Bota Šare

Tel: 020-754 482; www.bota-sare.hr

The island's renowned oysters figure prominently in this cavernous, stone-walled dining room with lots of outside tables on a waterside terrace. There is also a very good selection of seafood risotto, shellfish and pasta dishes as well as steaks. €€

Villa Koruna

Mali Ston bb; tel: 020-754 999; www.vila-koruna.hr

The best known of the Mali Ston restaurants, the Koruna has a vast, glass-covered terrace, a cosy, old-fashioned dining room, and fish swimming in large tanks (as well as two large turtles, which are not for clients' consumption). Presentation is great and the food is good, too. €€

NIGHTLIFE

Dubrovnik's nightlife tends to be concentrated on its many cafés and bars, rather than the sort of large beach clubs you find in other Croatian resorts. While there are a few nightclubs outside the edges of the Old Town, most people gather on the outdoor terraces of bars that fill the streets and squares. On warm evenings, you'll see people spilling out on to the steps of the narrow streets that lead to Prijeko off Stradun, as the tiny bars within will be packed within minutes.

The following listings are just a selection of the highlights of Dubrovnik's nightlife. For an overview of entertainment in the city, see page 22. Many of the bars and clubs are seasonal, with a fair number closing from early October and not reopening until Easter.

Concert venues

Lazareti
Frana Supila 8; tel: 020-324 633; www.lazareti.com
The 17th-century quarantine barracks just outside the City Walls is Dubrovnik's leading cultural and arts venue. It holds everything from folklore performances by Linđo Folklore Ensemble to underground club nights, mini festivals and outdoor film screenings. The complex also contains galleries and workshops.

Bars

Art Café
Branitelja Dubrovnika 25; tel: 020-311 097
Pull up a seat in one of the carved-out bathtubs in this funky bar a few minutes' walk from the Pile Gate. As it's so close to the university, it's a magnet for students.

La Bodega
Stradun; tel: 098-904 8469; www.labodega.hr
This smart bar is a lively and popular meeting point in the Stradun, where people share plates of *pršut* and cheese over drinks.

Buzz Bar
Prijeko 21; tel: 020-321 025
Set among Prijeko's touristy restaurants is this chilled-out bar with a bright modern interior and occasional live guitar sets.

D'Vino
Palmitoćeva 4a; tel: 020-321 1230; www.dvino.net
It's a tight squeeze in this busy wine bar off Stradun near the Pile Gate, where people are wedged into the narrow street enjoying excellent Croatian wines when they're not ensconced in the cosy vaulted interior.

Jazz Caffe Troubadour
Bunićeva Poljana 2; tel: 020-323 476
This Dubrovnik institution has a large

Stradun, the epicentre of Dubrovnik's nightlife

terrace in the shadow of the Cathedral, where live jazz (and music vaguely resembling jazz) is played on weekends.

Platanus Bar
Između Vrta 2; tel: 099-807 0742
There's a friendly vibe in this bar outside the Pile Gate that's more like a club, with themed nights and lots of dancing. Drinks are reasonably priced too.

Rock Caffe Exit
Boškovićeva 3; tel: 095-890 6472
You'll hear the music before you spot the subtle entrance to this cheerful bar off Stradun. The music might not be quite as rock as the name suggests, but the drinks are some of the cheapest in town.

Victoria Lounge Bar
tel: 020 440 588
The views of Dubrovnik's Old Town are sublime from the lounge bar of the Victoria restaurant at Villa Orsula hotel. It's one of the classiest places for a cocktail as you lounge on sofas on the large stone terrace overlooking the sea.

Clubs

Banje Beach Nightclub
Frana Supila 10/B, tel: 020-412 220;
www.banjebeach.com
The daytime atmosphere of this bar on Banje Beach becomes more sophisticated as the sun goes down and everyone grabs a cocktail. In the height of summer, it's open till 6am.

Culture Club Revelin
Ulica Svetog Dominika 3; tel: 020-436 010;
www.clubrevelin.com
The imposing fortress hosts club nights with international DJs and live bands. Clubbers can take a breather on the giant terrace with great views of the Old Town. During July, it attracts top names in electronic music for its annual Revelin Festival, as well as the Du-El-Fest electronic music festival in August.

Casinos

Merit Casino Libertas
Liechtensteinov put 3; tel: 091-632 1907;
www.meritcasinos.com
Dubrovnik's only casino is in the glittering setting of the five-star Hotel Rixos Libertas. You'll find the usual card tables, roulette, poker and slot machines along with a lounge bar.

Theatre

Marin Držić Theatre
Pred Dvorom 3; tel: 020-321 088
This neo-Renaissance theatre dating from 1865 is home to a repertory theatre company that stages Croatian and international productions. It's one of the main venues during the Summer Festival.

Cinema

Sloboda Cinema
Luža; tel: 020-321 425; www.kinematografi.org
Dubrovnik's only year-round cinema is right by the clock tower in Luža Square. Croatian films are screened as well as international releases, the latter with subtitles.

Dubrovnik's baroque cathedral

A–Z

A

Age restrictions

The age of consent in Croatia is 15. To drive legally in Croatia you must be at least 18 and have your full licence. Children under 12 are not allowed in the front seat of cars. The legal drinking age is 18.

B

Budgeting

Dubrovnik is one of Croatia's more expensive destinations. The following is a general guide to how to budget.

A glass of house wine will cost 10–20 kuna. A main course in a cheap restaurant is about 40–60 kuna, and in a more expensive restaurant will be about 80–190 kuna.

It can be difficult to find budget accommodation in Dubrovnik as more and more luxury hotels spring up. A double room in a cheap hotel will cost 500 kuna; a moderate hotel in high season is about 1,000 kuna, and the luxury hotels will be well in excess of 3,500 kuna.

Buses are reasonably cheap, with fares at 15 kuna if bought on the bus and 12 kuna if bought at a kiosk. Ferry tickets vary enormously, but usually start at 30 kuna. A taxi from the airport will cost 350 kuna.

The major museums and sites charge from 20 to 120 kuna, with discounts for students and children. Admission to churches is free.

If you plan to pack in a lot of sights and explore the area, then a Dubrovnik Card (www.dubrovnikcard.com) could be good value. Available for one, three and seven days, it gives you free public transport as well as free entry into the top attractions including the ramparts and the Rector's Palace. It's about 10 percent cheaper if you buy it online, and you also receive discounts in participating shops and restaurants.

C

Children

Most hotels, restaurants and cafés are very accommodating to families. In many places children under three can stay free, and discounts are often available for accommodation, travel and food for under-12s and even older teenagers. Beaches offer plenty of water-based activities for children and well as dry sporting facilities for older children. There are a few sandy beaches on some of the islands, but Dubrovnik's beaches are pebbly or rocky. If you don't bring swimming shoes, they're easily available in shops.

The areas with the biggest selection of family-friendly hotels is Lapad

The tranquil harbour

and Babin Kuk, which is also where the most extensive beach facilities are.

Clothing

Most styles of dressing are tolerated, but Croatians like to dress smartly and you will blend in more easily if you do too. Visitors of both sexes should avoid short shorts and bare shoulders when visiting churches. Topless bathing is not actually forbidden on most beaches but it is not common. There is, however, a naturist beach on the island of Lokrum. For comfort, wear loose, light clothes in summer, but remember that sudden downpours do happen. A waterproof and umbrella are useful, as is a sweater or jacket for evenings. Flip-flop sandals, sunhats, sarongs and other beach cover-ups are easy to find when you get here.

Crime and safety

Dubrovnik is, on the whole, a safe city, and crime rates are low. As elsewhere, of course, take care of your property, keep an eye on your luggage, and don't flash large sums of money around. If you are a victim of a crime, report it to the police (tel: 192). You will need a police report, made within 24 hours, if you want to make an insurance claim.

Customs

Visitors from EU countries have no limits on what they can import, as long as they can prove it is for personal use. Visitors from outside the EU can bring two litres of table wine, two litres of liqueur or dessert wine, 1 litre of spirits, 200 cigarettes or 100 cigarillos or 50 cigars or 250g of tobacco into Croatia duty free. If you are carrying more than at total of €10,000 in cash or cheques, you must declare it at customs.

Disabled travellers

The smooth marble streets of the old town make it easy for people in wheelchairs to explore the old town. Many hotels have been updated to include facilities for people with disabilities, and there is a wheelchair-accessible public toilet at Pile Gate. People with limited mobility will find it difficult to climb the steps to the higher street and to walk the ramparts. However, there is a transporter that can be booked in advance (tel: 098-915 2834).

Embassies and consulates

The UK has the only English-speaking consulate in Dubrovnik.
Great Britain: Vukovarska 22; tel: 020-324 597

Electricity

The standard is 220 volts. Sockets take plugs with two round pins, so UK visitors need adapters. Visitors from the US and Canada need transformers for 110-volt appliances.

Resting near the Large Fountain of Onofrio

Emergency numbers

General emergency number: 112
Ambulance and medical emergency: 194
Fire service: 193
Police: 192
Assistance on the roads: 1987
Search and rescue at sea: 195

Etiquette

Croatians tend to be quite reserved with strangers. When addressing strangers, it is polite to use the honorific *gospodine* (for a man), *gospođo* (for a married woman) or *gospođice* (for a young unmarried woman).

Festivals

2–3 February: celebrations in honour of Sveti Vlaho (St Blaise).
Mid- to late February: Carnival, with colourful processions in Stradun and masked balls in the large hotels. Processions are also held in Cavtat.
March–April: Good Friday processions. Easter Sunday: processions after Mass and the blessing of the town at the land and sea gates.
Mid-May: Night of Museums.
Mid-June: Corpus Christi celebrated with Mass and street processions, Ana in the City Festival
Mid-July–late August: Dubrovnik Summer Festival.
July–August: Cavtat Summer Festival: male voice choirs and water polo tourna-

ments, Maraton Ladja annual boat race.
29 July: St Theodor's Day in Korčula is celebrated with the Moreška (Sword Dance Festival).
Early August: Southern Dalmatia Yacht Regatta, a two-day event.
Mid-September: Epidaurus Festival (music, art, drama) in Cavtat.
Late September–early October: Grape harvest festival in Pelješac and Korčula, Ston Wall Marathon in Ston
Late October: Semper Primus Rowing Regatta, Gruž Harbour. Dubrovnik Film Festival.G

Health

There are no particular health hazards in Croatia, and no vaccinations are required. Dubrovnik's tap water is safe to drink and it tastes fine, but bottled water *(voda)* is widely available if you prefer it. Mosquitoes can be a problem in summer, so take protective cream or lotion and perhaps invest in an appliance that plugs into a socket in your hotel room.

Citizens of Britain, Ireland and most European countries are entitled to free medical care, and don't forget take your EHIC (European Health Insurance Card) with you. However, it is advisable to take out a separate travel insurance policy as the EHIC doesn't cover repatriation costs.

Hospitals

Dubrovnik's hospital is in Lapad at Roka Mišetića, tel: 020-431 777, and has a

Lace stall

24-hour emergency department (tel: 194).

There is also the Policlinic, at Ante Starčevića 45, tel: 020-400 500; open Mon–Fri 8am–8pm, Sat 8am–1pm. There is also a dental surgery at Ul. Iva Vojnovića 30, tel: 020-333 417.

Hotel receptionists will be able to advise you about medical and dental services for non-urgent matters.

Chemists

There are chemists (*ljekarne*) all over the city. Main ones include:

Ljekarna Gruž, Obala Pape Ivana Pavle II 9, tel: 020-418 990; open Monday–Friday 7am–8pm, Saturday 7.30am–3pm.

Ljekarna Kod Zvonika, Placa, tel: 020-321 133; open Monday–Friday 7am–8pm, Saturday 7.30am–3pm.

Ljekarna Kod Male Braće, Placa 30, tel: 020-321 411; open Monday–Friday 7am–8.30pm, Saturday 7.30am–1.30pm.

Ljekarna Lapad, Mata Vodopića 30, tel: 020-436 788; open Monday–Friday 7am–8pm, Saturday 7.30am–3pm.

Kod Zvonika and Gruž are the rota chemists on duty alternately outside the above hours, but only 7.30am–8pm.

Hours and holidays

Most shops open Mon–Sat 9am–8pm in summer, although some close on Saturday afternoon. In winter, they may close for lunch. Supermarkets stay open till 9pm and also open on Sunday. Most markets operate from around 7am until noon or 1pm. Main post offices are open Mon–Fri 8am–7pm, Sat 8am–noon. Hours for larger banks are Mon–Fri 8am–7pm, Sat 8am–noon.

Public Holidays

1 January New Year's Day
6 January Epiphany
3 February Sveti Vlaho (St Blaise)
March/April Easter Monday
1 May Labour Day
June Corpus Christi (dates vary)
22 June Anti-Fascist Resistance Day
25 June Statehood Day
5 August Homeland Thanksgiving Day
15 August Feast of the Assumption
8 October Independence Day
1 November All Saints' Day
25–26 December Christmas

I

Internet facilities

There are numerous internet cafés in Dubrovnik, and hourly rates for internet access are about 25 kuna. Most hotels have WiFi, as do many bars and cafés, so don't hesitate to ask for the code if you're eating or drinking there.

L

LGBTQ travellers

Croatia is a Roman Catholic country, and homosexuality is tolerated but not embraced. The gay scene in Dubrovnik is minimal in spite of the fact that it's a popular destination for LGBTQ travel-

Street musicians on Stradun

lers. Caffe Troubadour in the old town is a popular meeting point, as is the nudist beach on the island of Lokrum. A useful guide to gay-friendly venues is www.croatia-gay.com.

M

Media

Online English-language newspapers include the *Dubrovnik Times* (www.dubrovacki.hr), which covers the city specifically, and *Croatia Times* (www.croatia-times.com).

Money

Currency

Croatia's currency is the kuna (abbreviated to kn or, sometimes, HRK), which is divided into 100 lipa. There are 1, 2, 5, 10, 20, 50 lipa coins, 1, 2, 5 and 25 kuna coins and 5, 10, 20, 50, 100, 200, 500 and 1,000 kuna banknotes. A few businesses will accept euros but give you back change in kunas and rarely at a favourable rate.

Changing money

Foreign currency can be exchanged at banks, exchange bureaux, post offices and most tourist agencies and hotels. Banking hours are Monday–Friday 8am–7pm (8am–5pm for smaller branches), Saturday 8am–noon/1pm.

Credit and debit cards

Most hotels, restaurants and larger shops accept credit cards, but it is always wise to check in advance. Cash machines (ATMs) are found throughout the city, especially in Stradun, and in Cavtat and Korčula, but are harder to find on the smaller islands.

Taxes

All prices shown are net, ie what you actually have to pay. If you look closely you may see that an amount for VAT (PDF) is detailed on some bills, but this does not mean it is extra, as the tax is built into the price.

Tipping

Service charge is rarely added to restaurant bills, so a tip of 10 percent could be added if you are happy with the service. In cheaper restaurants, you can just leave any coins from the change. For taxi drivers, just round up the amount. Hotel porters should be tipped if they are helpful, and cleaning staff should be given an amount commensurate with your length of stay.

P

Post

The main post offices (*pošta*) are in Široka 8 (off Stradun), open Mon–Fri 8am–7pm, Sat 8am–noon; and Vukovarska 16, open Mon–Fri 7am–8pm, Sat 8am–3pm. Stamps are sold in post offices and in some shops that sell postcards. It usually takes about two weeks for a postcard to get from Dubrovnik to another European destination, but it can be faster.

Sponza Palace

R

Religion

Croatia is an overwhelmingly Roman Catholic country, although there is a small minority of Muslims and Serbian Orthodox residents in Dubrovnik. There is also a tiny Jewish population in the city.

S

Smoking

There is a smoking ban on all enclosed public places including bars, restaurants and cafés. However, be prepared for plenty of smoke in outdoor terraces of cafés and restaurants.

T

Telephones

The prefix for Croatia is +385. The code for Dubrovnik and Southern Dalmatia is 020. To call Croatia from outside the country, first dial your international access code followed by the code for Croatia. When calling from abroad, omit the initial 0 in the regional access code. Directory enquiries: 11888. General information: 18981. International directory assistance: 11802

Public phones can be used only with phone cards, which can be bought in post offices and at newsagents' kiosks. You can make international calls from a phone box but it may be preferable to phone from a post office where you make your call then pay afterwards.

Mobile phone numbers begin with 09. As of 2017, EU roaming charges have been abolished so if you are living in the UK you will not be charged extra for using your data allowance in Croatia.

Time zones

Croatia follows Central European Time (GMT+1). From the last Sunday in March to the last Sunday in October, clocks are advanced one hour (GMT+2).

Toilets

There are public toilets in the old town, but they cost at least 10 kuna. Owners of bars and cafés won't be pleased if you use the facilities without buying a drink, and some need a key or a code. The only free public toilet is on the City Walls.

Tourist information

The main tourist offices are at Brsalje 5, just up from the Pile Gate (tel: 020-312 011), which is the most helpful. There is another in Gruž, at Obala Pape Ivana Pavla II 1 (tel: 020-417 983), and in Lapad, Kralja Tomislava 7 (020-437 460; open seasonally). Email for information: info@tzdubrovnik.hr.

Tours and guides

There are a number of tour agencies that organise trips to the Elaphite Islands, to Korčula, Ston and the Pelješac peninsula, to the Neretva River delta, to Mljet, and further afield to Montenegro, Mostar, Sarajevo and other destinations.

Atlas (www.atlas-croatia.com), the best known, has its main office on Lokrumska 1 (tel: 020-642 286; www.atlas-croatia.com). Elite Travel (Vukovarska 17, tel: 020-358 200, www.elite.hr) runs a similar programme with similar prices and does day cruises on the lovely galleon *Tirena*. Amico Tours (Čubranovićeva 11a, tel: 91 4444 445, www.amico-tours.com) has an interesting programme, and Globtour Dubrovnik (Prijeko 12, tel: 020-321 599, www.globtour.com) also runs a variety of tours. Adriana Shipping Company (tel: 020-471 199; www.adriana-cavtat.hr) does Elaphite Islands trips and others along the Dubrovnik Riviera (Lokrum, Mlini, Plat, Cavtat) on attractive old-style sailing boats.

Insight Guides (www.insightguides.com) offers a selection of tailor-made trips to Dubrovnik, including a sailing trip along Croatia's stunning Adriatic coast.

Transport

Arrival by air

From the UK, flights take about 2 hour 40 minutes. In summer there are frequent direct flights with British Airways (tel: 0844 493 0787, www.ba.com), Croatia Airlines (tel: 020-8563 0022, www.croatiaairlines.com), easyJet (tel: 0330 365 5000, www.easyjet.com), and Jet2 (tel: 0800 408 1350, www.jet2.com). There are a number of charter flights from holiday companies including Tui (tel: 0203-636 1931, www.tui.co.uk).

There are no direct flights from Australia, Canada or the US, but flights via London or other European airports are not hard to arrange.

Dubrovnik's airport (Zračna Luka; tel: 020-773 100, www.airport-dubrovnik.hr) is at Čilipi, about 20km (12 miles) south. Atlas Travel Agency runs a bus service between the airport and the main bus station that connects with the arrival of scheduled flights (40 kuna one way, 70 kuna return). The buses are very straightforward, efficient and take about 30 minutes to reach Pile Gate. You can take a taxi (about 300–350 kuna), but bear in mind that the driver won't be able to drop you off anywhere inside the old town.

Arrival by road

Many drivers take on the Adriatic Highway (Jadranska Magistrala), a breathtaking route that hugs the Adriatic coast. It's also impossibly busy in summer. A more practical route is the A1 two-lane motorway that is further inland and is getting extended all the time towards Dubrovnik.

Public transport

Buses. Dubrovnik's bus service, run by Libertas (tel: 0800 1910, www.libertas-dubrovnik.hr), is excellent, and unless you are out very late at night is probably the only form of transport you will need in the city. The Libertas kiosks at the bus station (Autobusni Kolodvor) on Put Republike, at the city end of Gruž Harbour and at the bus stops by Pile Gate, will provide you with an up-to-date timetable, as will the tourist office and most

The small but perfectly formed harbour at Šipan

hotel reception desks. You can pay on the bus (exact money only, currently 15 kuna), but it's cheaper and easier to buy tickets at newsagents kiosks (there's usually one near main bus stops) or at your hotel. You can buy any number you want, pay 12 kuna each and avoid the necessity of finding the right change. For many visitors, the No.6 is the most useful route, as it runs from Pile Gate to Lapad and Babin Kuk, where many hotels are located. The service runs about six times an hour at peak periods, and continues until 1am (later in high summer).

Long-distance buses – to Zagreb, Zadar, Split and international destinations – run from a bus station on Gruž Harbour (past the ferry terminal; tel: 060 30 50 70).

Boats. There are numerous boat services to the nearby islands and to Cavtat. For boats to Cavtat and Lokrum, simply turn up at the Old Port and you will have a choice of vessels of various shapes and sizes, all charging about the same fare. Nova International (tel: 020-313 599) runs fast services between Gruž and the Old Port, from Gruž to Zaton, and from the Old Port to Cavtat and the Elaphite Islands. For the Elaphites you can book trips through a number of different agencies, which have stands on Lapad Bay and in the Old Port. There is also a boat that shuttles across the harbour between Gruž and Lapad during the summer months.

There is a high-speed service that runs from Split to Dubrovnik, stopping at Hvar and Korčula, run by UTC Kapetan Luka (tel: 021-645 476; www.krilo.hr).

The service between Bari in Italy and Dubrovnik is run by Jadrolinja (www.jadro-linija.hr).

Taxis. Taxi fares are metered and are not exorbitant. There are taxi stands outside Pile Gate (which lists prices to major destinations), outside Ploče Gate, at Gruž Harbour (in front of the Jadrolinija office) and by the bus station. Radio Taxi Dubrovnik runs a 24-hour service (tel: 0 98 725 769). Taxi meters must be running for the fare to be valid, so double check before you go very far.

Driving

Unless you are visiting Dubrovnik as part of an extended tour of Croatia, travelling by car is not a good option. Cars are not allowed into the Old Town and parking in the New Town can be difficult. However, if you do travel by car try to find a hotel with private parking, and leave your car there when you arrive, or stay outside the town in Cavtat or Zaton and makes trips in by bus or boat.

If you are driving, remember to drive on the right and stick to the speed limits of 130kph (80mph) on motorways, 100kph (62mph) on dual carriageways, 50kph (30mph) in built-up areas and 80kph (50mph) outside built-up areas, or you could risk a heavy fine. Police are also clamping down on drink-driving.

Car and scooter rental. If you want to hire a car to make trips outside the city, you could book in advance by checking www.carrentals.co.uk, which lists the best deals from a huge number of companies.

Driving through the heartland

Europcar has an office at Dubrovnik airport (tel: 098- 231 079), Hertz is at Frana Supila 9 (tel: 020-425 000) and Gulliver (a reliable local company) is at Obala Stjepana Radića 25 (tel: 020-410 888; www.gulliver.hr). Avis also has an office at the airport (tel: 913 143 019) which it shares with Budget and in town at Kardinala Stepinca 60 (tel: 959 222 333). Brabel at Iva Vojnovića 75 (tel: tel: 020-323 333; www.brabel.hr) also has scooter and motorcycle rental.

Parking. There is a 24-hour car park outside the Old Town at Ilijina Glavica, and at Gruž Harbour, which charges 10 kuna an hour or a daily rate of 100 kuna. The car park is Gruž is very convenient if you plan to take a ferry journey from the harbour. There are smaller car parks outside the Old Town, which are payable by parking vouchers bought at newspaper kiosks, at parking meters (exact change) and via SMS message on mobile phones.

Petrol. There's one petrol station between Gruž and the Old Town on Ulica Vladimira Nazora open 24 hrs daily, and one on Obala Lapadska beside Lapad harbour (weekdays 7am–7pm, Sun and holidays 7am–1pm).

Travel outside Croatia

Visiting Montenegro. Visitors to Dubrovnik have the opportunity of a day excursion to the Bay of Kotor (Boka Kotorska), which lies just over the border in Montenegro 40km (25 miles) to the south. A Unesco World Heritage Site, the huge Kotor Fjord is a sunken river canyon, 28km (16 miles) long and 30 metres (100ft) deep, with four distinct bays. It is a breathtaking sight, especially for anyone arriving by boat. The bay has a number of beaches, resorts and small islands, and much of the ancient architecture in the fishing and boat-building villages is from the Venetian period.

The airport for the region is 4km (2.5 miles) outside Tivat, a largely 19th-century town in the southernmost bay. The naval base built by the Austrians is in private hands and has been turned into Porto Montenegro, with hundreds of berths for super-yachts and the depressing ambition of becoming the Monaco of the Adriatic.

Beaches and resorts continue down the coast to the Budva Riviera (Budvanska rivijera), 11km (7 miles) of fine sandy beaches. Its beauty is at great risk of being eroded, sadly, as development has been racing along at dizzying speed. Construction cranes are a ubiquitous sight as foreign buyers – usually Russian, judging from the advertising hoardings – fill every available space. Budva does have a very attractive walled old town, though, which was almost entirely rebuilt after an earthquake in 1978.

Montenegro's capital, Podgorica, is a modern, workmanlike city of around 165,000. Much of it was destroyed in World War II, but there is still an old Turkish quarter and some interesting restored churches. The city has an active cultural life, and socialising takes place out of doors in the main square, Trg Republike.

Montenegro's old royal capital is Cetinje, on the inland road between

Mljet lake scene

Podgorica and Kotor, and it remains the country's cultural and educational centre. Its museums and galleries provide an idea of Montenegro and its past. These include an art museum with the most valuable murals in Montenegro. Icons can also be seen in the Museum of Cetinje Monastery. The National Museum is housed in the palace of Nikola I Petrović-Njegoš, Montenegro's only king, who reigned 1910–18.

Trips can be made independently if you hire a car, which is easy to take into Montenegro. Tour companies such as Viator (www.viator.com) organise day trips that usually include Kotor, Cetinje and Budva. There are buses that go to the main towns in Montenegro, but their schedules don't leave much flexibility if you want to see more than one place in a day.

Villa/apartment rentals

Numerous companies offer rentals in villas and apartments to suit most budgets, ranging from small flats in the Old Town to large villas in the surrounding countryside. Here is a selection:

Croatian Villa Holidays; tel: +44 (0) 1494 671359; www.croatianvillaholidays.com.

Croatian Villas; tel: +44 (0) 20 8888 6655; www.croatianvillas.com.

Holiday Lettings; tel: +44 (0) 1865 312000; www.holidaylettings.co.uk.

HomeAway; tel: +44 (0) 20 8827 1971; www.homeaway.co.uk.

Olivers Travels; tel: +44 (0) 800 133 7999; www.oliverstravels.com.

Owners Direct; tel: +44 (0) 20 8827 1998; www.ownersdirect.co.uk.

Rose of Dubrovnik: tel: +385 (0) 91 596 7508; www.dubrovnikapartmentsvillas.com.

Visas and passports

Citizens of EU countries, and those from Australia, New Zealand, the US and Canada, need only a valid passport to visit Croatia for stays of up to three months. If you are going on day trips to Bosnia-Herzegovina or Montenegro you need to take your passport with you, but you don't need a visa.

All foreign visitors are required to register with the police within 24 hours of their arrival, but in practice this is done by the hotel or owner of the private accommodation in which you are staying, and it is their responsibility, not yours, to see that it is done.

Weights and measures

Croatia uses the metric system.

Websites

Useful websites include: www.tzdubrovnik.hr; www.frankabout croatia.com; www.buscroatia.com; www.visit-croatia.co.uk

Women travellers

Female travellers do not usually experience harassment in Dubrovnik, and anyone making unwanted advances will generally take a firm no for an answer.

Most restaurants in Dubrovnik will have menus in English

LANGUAGE

Croatian is a difficult language to grasp; it's an inflected language with seven cases and complicated grammar. And the Dalmatian dialect often creeps into conversation, which can cause extra confusion. Although most people in the tourism industry in Dubrovnik speak English very well, a few words of Croatian are appreciated in the rural regions.

Pronunciation tips

Croatians use a customised version of the Roman alphabet, with the pronunciation of many letters being the same in Croatian and English. Every single letter is pronounced and their sounds do not change from word to word.

c like the 'ts' in 'hats'
ć like the 'tu' in 'nature'
č like the 'ch' in 'chip'
đ like the 'du' in 'endure' (sometimes written dj if the correct character is unavailable)
dž like the 'j' in 'juice'
j like the 'y' in 'yacht'
lj like the 'lli' in 'billion'
nj like the 'ny' in 'banyan'
š like the 'sh' in 'lush'
ž like the 's' in 'treasure'

Useful phrases

Hello *Bok*
Good morning. *Dobro jutro.*
Good day/afternoon. *Dobar dan.*
Good evening. *Dobra večer.*
Good night. *Laku noć.*
Goodbye. *Do viđenja.*
Welcome. *Dobro došli.*
My name is … *Moje ime je …*
How are you? *Kako ste?*
Yes *da*
No *ne*
Where? When? How? *Gdje? Kada? Kako?*
How much? *Koliko?*
Thank you. *Hvala.*
Please *molim*
Excuse me, please. *Oprostite, molim.*
Do you speak (English, German, Italian, Croatian)? *Govorite li (engleski, njemački, talijanski, hrvatski)?*
I (don't) speak *(Ne) govorim*
I (don't) understand *(Ne) razumijem*
Cheers *živjeli*

Somewhere to stay

Can you recommend…? *Možete li preporučiti…?*
a hotel *hotel*
a hostel *hostel*
a campsite *kamp*
a bed and breakfast *polupansion*
What is it near? *Što se nalazi u blizini?*
How do I get there? *Kako mogu stići tamo?*

At the hotel

Do you have …? *Imate li… ?*

a room *sobu*
a single room *jednokrevetnu sobu*
a double room *dvokrevetnu sobu*
with a shower/bath *sa tušem/banjom*
one night/week *jednu noć/tjedan*
Bed and breakfast *noćenje i doručak*
Full board/half board *pansion/polu-pansion*
How much is it …? *Koliko košta za …?*
per night *jednu noć*
per person *po osobi*
balcony *balkon*
terrace *terasa*
Is there anything cheaper? *Ima li nešto jeftinije?*
When's check-out? *Kada moramo napustiti?*
Can I leave this in the safe? *Mogu li ostaviti ovo u sefu?*
Can I leave my bags? *Mogu li ostaviti torbe?*
Can I have my bill/ a receipt? *Mogu li dobiti račun/priznanicu?*
I'll pay in cash/by credit card. *Plaćam gotovinom/kreditnom karticom.*

At the bar/restaurant

Restaurant *restoran*
Breakfast *doručak*
Lunch *ručak*
Coffee house *kavana*
Drink *piće*
One portion *jednu porciju*
Have you got a table for …? *Imate li stol za … osobe?*
May I have the menu (wine list)? *Molim vas jelovnik (vinsku kartu)?*
Have you got any food for vegetari-ans? *Imate li nešto za vegetarijance?*
Thank you, it was delicious *bilo je jako dobro*
The bill, please *račun molim*
Beer *pivo*
Black coffee *crna kava*
Brandy *rakija*
Fruit juice *voćni sok*
Mineral water *mineralna voda*
Plum brandy *šljivovica*
Table wine *stolno vino*
Tea (with milk/lemon, rum) *čaj (s mlijekom/s limunom/s rumom)*
Wine (white, red, rosé) *vino (bijelo, crno, roze)*
Bread *kruh*
Cheese *sir*
Cold meat *hladno pečenje*
Ham (raw, cooked, smoked) *šunka (sirova, kuhana, dimljena)*
Olives *masline*
Soup *juha*
Beefsteak *biftek*
Chicken *pile*
Pork chops *svinjski kotleti*
Lamb on the spit *janje na ražnju*
Turkey *tuka*
Veal cutlet *teleći odrezak*
Cucumber *krastavac*
Green pepper *paprika*
Mushrooms *gljive*
Onion *luk*
Potato *krumpir*
Salad *salata*
Cake *kolač*
Fruit salad *voćna salata*
Ice cream *sladoled*
Pancakes *palačinke*

Konoba sign

Numbers

0 *nula*
1 *jedan*
2 *dva*
3 *tri*
4 *četiri*
5 *pet*
6 *šest*
7 *sedam*
8 *osam*
9 *devet*
10 *deset*
11 *jedanaest*
12 *dvanaest*
20 *dvadeset*
30 *trideset*
40 *četrdeset*
50 *pedeset*
60 *šezdeset*
70 *sedamdeset*
80 *osamdeset*
90 *devedeset*
100 *sto*
1,000 *tisuću*

Getting around

Where is the …? *Gdje je …?*
railway station? *željeznička postaja?*
bus stop? *autobusna postaja?*
What time does the … leave? *U koliko sati polazi …?*
train/bus/ferry? *vlak/autobus/trajekt?*
one way/return ticket *jednosmjerna/ povratna karta*
Booking *rezervacija*
Airport *zračna luka*
Timetable *raspored*

How much is the ticket to …? *Koliko košta karta za …?*

Shopping

Do you have …? *Imate li …?*
How much is it …? *Kolika košta …?*
Bakery *pekara*
Butchers *mesnica*
Department store *robna kuća*
Grocer *dućan*
Laundry *praonica rublja*
Market *tržnica*
Pastry shop *slastičarnica*
Supermarket *samoposluživanje*
Price *cijena*
Cheap *jeftino*
Expensive *skupo*

Money

Where's…? *Gdje je…?*
the ATM *bankomat*
the bank *banka*
the currency exchange office *mjenjačnica*
What time does the bank open/ close? *Kada se banka otvara/zatvara?*
I'd like to change some dollars/ pounds into kuna. *Htio m/Htjela f bih promijeniti dolare/funte u kune.*

Telephone

A phone card/prepaid phone, please *Telefonsku karticu/Prepaid telefon, molim Vas.*
How much? *Koliko*
Can I recharge/buy minutes for this phone? *Mogu li napuniti/kupiti nadoplatni bon za ovaj telefon?*

Mushrooms for sale — *Bar Massimo*

Where's the pay phone? *Gdje je telefonska govornica?*

What's the area/country code for...? *Koji je regionalni/državni pozivni broj za...?*

What's the number for Information? *Koji je broj informacija?*

I'd like the number for... *Htio m/Htjela f bih broj za...*

I'd like to call collect [reverse the charges]. *Htio m/Htjela f bih nazvati na račun primatelja poziva.*

My phone doesn't work here. *Moj telefon ne radi ovdje.*

What network are you on? *Na kojoj si mreži?*

Is it 3G? *Je li to 3G?*

I have run out of credit/minutes. *Nemam više kredita/minuta.*

Can I buy some credit? *Mogu li kupiti nadoplatni bon?*

Do you have a phone charger? *Imate li punjač za mobitel?*

Can I have your number? *Mogu li dobiti vaš broj?*

Here's my number. *To je moj broj.*

Please call/text me. *Molim Vas nazovite me/napišite mi poruku.*

I'll call you. *Nazvat ću Vas*

I'll text you. *Napisat ću Vam poruku.*

Online

Where's an internet café? *Gdje ima internet cafe?*

Does it have wireless internet? *Ima li bežični internet?*

What is the WiFi password? *Koja je lozinka za bežičnu mrežu?*

Is the WiFi free? *Je li bežična mreža besplatna?*

What's your email? *Koja je vaša e-mail adresa?*

My email is... *Moja e-mail adresa je...*

Can I...? *Mogu li...?*

use any computer *koristiti bilo koji računar*

access the internet *pristupiti internetu*

check my email *provjeriti e-mail*

print *printati*

plug in/charge my laptop/iPhone/iPad? *uključiti/napuniti svoj laptop/iPhone/iPad?*

access Skype? *Mogu li koristiti Skype?*

Social media

Are you on Facebook/Twitter? *Jesi li na Facebooku/Twitteru?*

What's your username? *Koje ti je korisničko ime?*

I'll add you as a friend. *Dodat ću te za prijatelja.*

I'll follow you on Twitter. *Slijedit ću te na Twitteru.*

I'll put the pictures on Facebook/Twitter. *Stavit ću slike na Facebook/Twitter.*

Game of Thrones is partly filmed in Dubrovnik

BOOKS AND FILM

Dubrovnik received an unexpected boost in 2010 when the city became the setting for the HBO television series *Game of Thrones*, subsequently attracting a new generation of visitors. But the history of Dubrovnik is considerably more dramatic than anything that the HBO producers can dream up. Because the more recent events of the 1990s Homeland War are often baffling to visitors, some background reading would help to put the city's modern history into context.

Books

History

Dubrovnik: A History by Robin Harris. A detailed, weighty, but accessible history of the city.

The National Question in Yugoslavia by Ivo Banac. An examination of the tension between Serbian nationalism, Croatian nationalism and Yugoslavianism in the Balkans from the mid-19th century to the 1921 Vidovdan Constitution.

The Balkans 1804–1999: Nationalism, War and the Great Powers by Misha Glenny. An ambitious attempt to explain the history of the Balkans and how the rest of the world meddled in its affairs.

The Impossible Country: A Journey Through the Last Days of Yugoslavia by Brian Hall. An engrossing account of the author's journey during the last days of Yugoslavia in 1991.

The Death of Yugoslavia by Laura Silber and Alan Little. A riveting account of the events that contributed to the 1991 war and running on to the Dayton Accord, presented from a historical perspective.

Croatia: A Nation Forged in War by Marcus Tanner. This is a compelling account of Croatian history, from the Greeks and Romans to the present day.

The Demise of Yugoslavia: A Political Memoir by Stjepan Mesić. Insightful account of the collapse of the former Yugoslavia written by the federation's last president, and the first democratically elected president of independent Croatia.

The Yugoslav Auschwitz and the Vatican: The Croatian Massacre of the Serbs During World War II by Vladimir Dedijer. Written by a former Yugoslav ambassador to the UN, this impeccably researched book covers a secret episode of the 20th century and one that many Croatians – and Roman Catholics – would prefer had remained secret.

How We Survived Communism and Even Laughed by Slavenka Drakulić. Essays on life under Communism.

Balkan Express by Slavenka Drakulić. A compelling insight, given through a series of essays, into the effects of the Homeland War on the lives of ordinary people.

Balkan Ghosts: A Journey Through History by Robert D. Kaplan. A brilliant take on the 20th-century history of the Balkans by an American war reporter.

Game of Thrones' Queen Cersei Lannister

Croatia Through History by Branka Magaš. Despite being Croatian, historian and journalist Branka Magaš bravely attempts to cover objectively the history of Croatia from the Middle Ages to the present and does it remarkably well.

Croatia: A History by Ivo Goldstein. An authoritative history of the country by a professor at Zagreb University.

Gastronomy

A Taste of Croatia: Savoring the Food, People and Traditions of Croatia's Adriatic Coast by Karen Evenden. Not so much a cookbook as a well-written and lengthy love letter celebrating its subject.

My Favourite Croatian Recipes by Sandra Lougher. One of very few books about Croatian food in English.

The Best of Croatian Cooking – Expanded Edition by Liliana Pavičić and Gordana Pirker-Mosher. As well as 200 recipes, there is an introduction covering Croatia's culinary tradition and local specialities and a useful wine guide.

Travel

Croatia: Travels in Undiscovered Country by Tony Fabijančić. A travelogue written by a Canadian-born son of Croatian immigrants who explores the back roads of his ancestral homeland.

Black Lamb and Grey Falcon by Rebecca West. West's colossal and seminal account of several journeys through Yugoslavia during the 1930s remains essential reading to anyone who wants a deeper understanding of Balkan history.

Chasing a Croatian Girl by Cody Brown. A witty tale of an American professor at Zagreb University who falls in love with a Croatian girl, a relationship that becomes a window into Croatia's culture.

Fiction

The Museum of Unconditional Surrender by Dubravka Ugrešić. A novel that weaves humour and bitterness honing in on the life of a 45-year-old Croatian woman living in exile.

Croatian Nights ed. Borivoj Radaković, Matt Thorne and Tony White. An eclectic but brilliant collection of short stories by Croatian and British writers, which grew out of a movement called FAK – Festival of Alternative Literature.

Television and Film

Game of Thrones: Several series of HBO's incredibly popular fantasy drama set in the Middle Ages have been filmed in Dubrovnik, the fictional King's Landing.

Cure: The Life of Another (2014) Dubrovnik just after the 1991–92 siege is the setting for this unsettling thriller about two teenage girls.

Penelope (2009) Filmed in Dubrovnik, this Croatian-Australian co-production takes the woman's point of view in Homer's *Odyssey*, as long-suffering Penelope waits for her husband Odysseus to return.

The Secret Invasion (1964) Roger Corman's low-budget version of *The Dirty Dozen* takes place in Dubrovnik as a group of men stage a daring mission in Nazi-occupied Yugoslavia.

ABOUT THIS BOOK

This *Explore Guide* has been produced by the editors of Insight Guides, whose books have set the standard for visual travel guides since 1970. With top-quality photography and authoritative recommendations, these guidebooks bring you the very best routes and itineraries in the world's most exciting destinations.

BEST ROUTES

The routes in the book provide something to suit all budgets, tastes and trip lengths. As well as covering the destination's many classic attractions, the itineraries track lesser-known sights, and there are also excursions for those who want to extend their visit outside the city. The routes embrace a range of interests, so whether you are an art fan, a gourmet, a history buff or have kids to entertain, you will find an option to suit.

We recommend reading the whole of a route before setting out. This should help you to familiarise yourself with it and enable you to plan where to stop for refreshments – options are shown in the 'Food and Drink' box at the end of each tour.

For our pick of the tours by theme, consult Recommended Routes for... (see pages 6–7).

INTRODUCTION

The routes are set in context by this introductory section, giving an overview of the destination to set the scene, plus background information on food and drink, shopping and more, while a succinct history timeline highlights the key events over the centuries.

DIRECTORY

Also supporting the routes is a Directory chapter, with a clearly organised A–Z of practical information, our pick of where to stay while you are there and select restaurant listings; these eateries complement the more low-key cafés and restaurants that feature within the routes and are intended to offer a wider choice for evening dining. Also included here are some nightlife listings, plus a handy language guide and our recommendations for books and films about the destination.

ABOUT THE AUTHORS

Mary Novakovich is an award-winning journalist and travel writer based in Hertfordshire. She has been visiting Croatia, where her parents were born, since the 1970s and goes back whenever humanly possible. When she's not updating guidebooks, she contributes regularly to British newspapers including *The Independent* and *The Guardian*.

CONTACT THE EDITORS

We hope you find this Explore Guide useful, interesting and a pleasure to read. If you have any questions or feedback on the text, pictures or maps, please do let us know. If you have noticed any errors or outdated facts, or have suggestions for places to include on the routes, we would be delighted to hear from you. Please drop us an email at hello@insightguides.com. Thanks!

914.972
INS
2018
(110)

CREDITS

Explore Dubrovnik
Editor: Carine Tracanelli
Author: Mary Novakovich
Head of Production: Rebeka Davies
Update Production: Apa Digital
Picture Editor: Tom Smyth
Cartography: updated by Carte
Photo credits: Alamy 40, 45L; AWL Images 4/5T, 8/9T; Bigstock 18; Borko Vukosav 100/101; Corbis 27; Corrie Wingate/Apa Publications 4ML, 4MC, 4MR, 4MR, 4MC, 4ML, 6BC, 8ML, 8MC, 8ML, 8MC, 8MR, 8MR, 15, 16, 16/17, 17L, 19, 20, 21, 24, 26, 28ML, 28MC, 81L, 80/81, 82, 83, 84MC, 101L, 118, 118/119, 119L; Dominic Burdon/APA Publications 6TL, 6MC, 7T, 7MR, 7MR, 13, 14, 24/25, 28ML, 28MC, 28MR, 28MR, 30, 32, 32/33, 33L, 38, 39L, 43, 66, 67, 78, 79, 80, 98/99, 100, 106, 107, 109, 114, 115; Esculap Restaurants 84MC, 96, 96/97, 97L, 98, 99L; Getty Images 10/11, 22, 28/29T, 36/37, 42, 44, 47, 48, 71, 74, 84/85T, 92/93, 102/103, 104/105; Goran Ergović/Croatian Tourist Board 25L; Hotel Stari Grad 86, 87, 94, 95; Importanne Resort 90, 90/91, 91L; iStock 1, 6ML, 7M, 12, 34, 38/39, 46, 52, 58/59, 60, 68, 68/69, 69L, 72/73, 84MR, 108, 110, 111, 116, 117; Leonardo 51, 88, 88/89, 89L; Mario Romulić & Dražen Stojčić/Croatian Tourist Board 84ML; Photoshot 44/45, 53, 56, 61, 70; Plazibat/Cropix/SIPA/REX/Shutterstock 120; Restaurant Zoë 84ML; Robert Harding 23, 30, 35, 41, 49, 50, 54/55, 57, 62, 63, 64/65, 76/77, 112/113; Stari Grad 84MR; Tonci Plazibat/Cropix/SIPA/Rex Features 121; Travel Pictures Ltd 75
Cover credits: Shutterstock (main); iStock (bottom)

Printed by CTPS – China

All Rights Reserved
© 2018 Apa Digital (CH) AG and
Apa Publications (UK) Ltd

Second Edition 2018

DISTRIBUTION

UK, Ireland and Europe
Apa Publications (UK) Ltd
sales@insightguides.com
United States and Canada
Ingram Publisher Services
ips@ingramcontent.com
Australia and New Zealand
Woodslane
info@woodslane.com.au
Southeast Asia
Apa Publications (Singapore) Pte
singaporeoffice@insightguides.com
Worldwide
Apa Publications (UK) Ltd
sales@insightguides.com

SPECIAL SALES, CONTENT LICENSING AND COPUBLISHING

Insight Guides can be purchased in bulk quantities at discounted prices. We can create special editions, personalised jackets and corporate imprints tailored to your needs.
sales@insightguides.com
www.insightguides.biz

INDEX

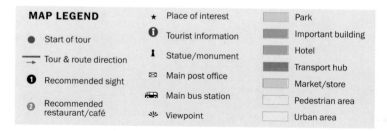

MAP LEGEND

- ● Start of tour
- → Tour & route direction
- ❶ Recommended sight
- ❷ Recommended restaurant/café

- ★ Place of interest
- ❶ Tourist information
- ⚊ Statue/monument
- ✉ Main post office
- 🚌 Main bus station
- ⚘ Viewpoint

- Park
- Important building
- Hotel
- Transport hub
- Market/store
- Pedestrian area
- Urban area

INSIGHT ⊙ GUIDES
OFF THE SHELF

Since 1970, INSIGHT GUIDES has provided a unique perspective on the world's best travel destinations by using specially commissioned photography and illuminating text written by local authors.

Whether you're planning a city break, a walking tour or the journey of a lifetime, our superb range of guidebooks and phrasebooks will inspire you to discover more about your chosen destination.

INSIGHT GUIDES

offer a unique combination of stunning photos, absorbing narrative and detailed maps, providing all the inspiration and information you need.

PHRASEBOOKS & DICTIONARIES

help users to feel at home, when away. Pocket-sized with a free app to download, they go where you do.

CITY GUIDES

pack hundreds of great photos into a smaller format with detailed practical information, so you can navigate the world's top cities with confidence.

EXPLORE GUIDES

feature easy-to-follow walks and itineraries in the world's most exciting destinations, with our choice of the best places to eat and drink along the way.

POCKET GUIDES

combine concise information on where to go and what to do in a handy compact format, ideal on the ground. Includes a full-colour, fold-out map.

EXPERIENCE GUIDES

feature offbeat perspectives and secret gems for experienced travellers, with a collection of over 100 ideas for a memorable stay in a city.

www.insightguides.com